Andrew Bradstock is Howard Paterson Professor of Theology and Public Issues at the University of Otago, New Zealand. He is the author and editor of several books in the field of radical religion and politics in seventeenth-century England, including *Faith in the Revolution: The Political Theologies of Müntzer and Winstanley* (1997), *Winstanley and the Diggers, 1649–1999* (2000) and – edited with Chris Rowland – *Radical Christian Writings: A Reader* (2002).

'Andrew Bradstock has balanced affection and scholarship in his splendid introduction to a social and religious world in which much is bizarrely different, but much is prophetic of modern spiritual and political explorations. It is a pity that contemporaries did not have such a clear and un-sensationalised guide to the radical religion of the Interregnum; it might have encouraged them not to subject James Nayler to bodily mutilation, flogging and perpetual imprisonment.'
– *Diarmaid MacCulloch, Professor of the History of the Church, University of Oxford and author of* A History of Christianity: The First Three Thousand Years

'The upheavals of the English civil war triggered an astonishing explosion of ideas – on religion, politics, society, economics and morality – that were unprecedented and without parallel in English history. These ideas crystallised in a succession of new movements: the pioneering democratic Levellers; communist Diggers; millenarian Fifth Monarchists, proclaiming an imminent kingdom of heaven on earth; and Quakers, fiery and combative evangelists who struck fear into most of their contemporaries. Andrew Bradstock brings these movements to vivid life, capturing their spirit and excitement, and explaining their ideas and appeal. He assesses, too, the challenge they presented to the government and to social order. His book provides an accessible, scholarly, and up-to-date introduction to all these groups, along with Baptists, Ranters and Muggletonians, and offers an ideal introduction for both undergraduates and general readers. Although most of these movements have long since vanished,

Bradstock spells out in a stimulating conclusion how many of the concerns they raised – on democracy, authority, toleration, property rights, and gender, for example – remain pressing issues today.'
– *Bernard Capp, FBA, Professor of History, University of Warwick*

'At the heart of this important book is Andrew Bradstock's concern with the "power of religious ideas to inspire political action" in the tumultuous years of the English revolution. He shows in lively and lucid prose how attacks on the established church and speculation about sin, salvation and religious truth had profound implications for seventeenth-century government and society. The writings, arguments and interventions of a remarkable array of individuals and movements are presented; Bradstock provides a balanced discussion of the latest scholarly debates on Quakers, Ranters, Levellers and the rest, but often he allows his subjects to speak for themselves with generous extracts from the vivid pamphlets in which positions were defended, and enemies denounced. The author covers inspirational but ephemeral movements, like the Diggers who, energised by the extraordinary prose of Gerrard Winstanley, sought to make the earth "a common treasury for all", and other groups like Quakers and Baptists, who endure to this day. Students, more advanced scholars and all those concerned with the dramatic conflicts and fundamental debates of seventeenth-century England will benefit enormously from Bradstock's book, and will be encouraged to reflect on the continuing relevance of his themes to contemporary concerns with religious freedom and social justice.'
– *Ann Hughes, Professor of Early Modern History, Keele University*

RADICAL RELIGION IN CROMWELL'S ENGLAND

A Concise History from the English Civil War to the End of the Commonwealth

ANDREW BRADSTOCK

I.B. TAURIS

LONDON · NEW YORK

For Chris Rowland

Published in 2011 by I.B.Tauris & Co Ltd
6 Salem Road, London W2 4BU
175 Fifth Avenue, New York NY 10010
www.ibtauris.com

Distributed in the United States and Canada Exclusively by Palgrave Macmillan
175 Fifth Avenue, New York NY 10010

International Library of Historical Studies, Vol 58

ISBN: 978 1 84511 764 1 (HB)
ISBN: 978 1 84511 765 8 (PB)

A full CIP record for this book is available from the British Library
A full CIP record is available from the Library of Congress

Library of Congress Catalog Card Number: available

Designed and typeset by 4word Ltd, Bristol
Printed and bound in Great Britain by TJ International, Padstow, Cornwall

Contents

List of Illustrations

1. A portrait of the Leveller leader John Lilburne at his trial for treason at the London Guildhall in October 1649. He holds a copy of Sir Edward Coke's 'Institutes of the Laws of England'.

   © The British Library Board, shelfmark C.37.d.51.(5)

2. The General Council of the Army, chaired by General Thomas Fairfax, meeting in 1647.

   © The British Library Board, shelfmark E 409/25

3. Thomas Rainsborough's famous contribution to the Putney Debates now immortalized in St Mary's Church.

   Photo: Paul Donnelly. By kind permission of St Mary's Church, Putney

4. A pamphlet hostile to the Ranters, published in 1650 during their period of greatest influence.

   © The British Library Board, shelfmark E 620.(2)

5. An anti-Quaker tract issued five years later. The same images have been used to attack both movements.

   © The British Library Board, shelfmark E 833.(14)

6. Women were allowed to preach at Quaker gatherings, and at some Baptist meetings, but they had many detractors, even within these movements.

© Mary Evans Picture Library

7. A depiction of the punishment meted out to Quaker leader, James Nayler, for the crime of riding into Bristol in imitation of the original Palm Sunday.

© The Trustees of the British Museum – reg. no. 1953,0411.61.

8. An engraved portrait of Lodowicke Muggleton from his autobiography 'The Acts of the Witnesses' published in 1699.

© The British Library Board, shelfmark 699.f.9.(1.)

9. Jerome Willis as General Thomas Fairfax in the 1975 film *Winstanley*, based on David Caute's novel, *Comrade Jacob* and produced by Kevin Brownlow and Andrew Mollo.

© The Kobal Collection/BFI

10. A memorial to Gerrard Winstanley installed in 2009 in the parish church of Cobham, Surrey, where he served for a time as a churchwarden.

Used by kind permission of David Taylor

11. The cast of the English Civil War drama *The Devil's Whore*, produced for Channel 4 by Company Pictures and screened in 2008.

© 2008, a Company Pictures production for Channel 4, directed by Peter Flannery

12. A demonstrator recalls Gerrard Winstanley's views on property outside the G20 world leaders summit in London in March 2009. The Digger leader was also quoted by Prime Minister Gordon Brown in a speech on the eve of the summit.

© MJ Kim/Getty Images for TVNZ

Preface and
Acknowledgements

Like many enthusiasts for the seventeenth-century 'radicals', my first encounter with most of them came via Christopher Hill's *The World Turned Upside Down*. I only met Dr Hill once, and we spent more time discussing cricket in his native Yorkshire than issues from an earlier century, but for all the inspiration, insight and sheer pleasure that his numerous books have given me I am truly thankful. I also wish to thank Denys Turner, who first enabled me to study the Levellers, Diggers and their contemporaries in a formal academic setting, and my subsequent research supervisors, David McLellan and Peter Matheson, for stimulating further my thinking about 'religious radicalism' and the historical movements and figures which embodied it. Another source of inspiration and encouragement has been Christopher Rowland – whose passion for the groups discussed here and commitment to discovering fresh insights into their work is totally infectious – and I express my gratitude to both Chris, and another fellow-toiler in the field, David Taylor, for their friendship and collaboration over many years.

For help and advice with specific sections of this book I thank my colleague at Otago, Tim Cooper, who teaches a popular undergraduate course on 'Ranters and Radicals' and whose kindness in introducing me to some recent literature, and reading some chapters in draft, has proved invaluable; and my friend and fellow Bristol alumnus Stephen Copson, a much-respected Baptist historian who kindly read and commented on part of this book in draft and alerted me to some scholarship I might otherwise have missed. I am also grateful to Jim Holstun, for his inspiration and encouragement over the years, and John Gurney, for the way that he has broadened our knowledge and understanding of the Diggers through his painstaking research. I have much valued the support and encouragement of my colleagues in the Department of Theology and Religion at Otago, and take this opportunity formally to thank them, as I do my editor at I.B.Tauris, Alex Wright, who conceived the idea of this book and whose enthusiasm for and belief in it has been so vital to its completion.

Few books are produced without some pain and sacrifice, as much on the part of those around the writer as the writer him- or herself. This has certainly been the case with this project, and for all her patience, long-suffering and resilience, not to mention practical help, advice and wisdom, I thank my wife and fellow voluntary exile, Helen. This really has been a shared endeavour.

In one sense I have been involved with the subject matter of this book all my life, having been raised in a Particular Baptist household and, like Gerrard Winstanley, 'gon through the ordinance of dipping' in my youth. Writing this book I have often thought back to the beliefs, practices and lifestyle of our chapel community back then in 1960s and 70s south London, marvelling how in so many ways we kept alive the traditions of our seventeenth-century Puritan forebears. If this means that, in a way of which most of the people in these pages would approve, I have been able to write on the basis of experience and not just book learning, I count that a huge privilege.

Dunedin

Introduction

IN APRIL 1999 several dozen lands-rights activists marched up a hill in the stockbroker belt of Surrey and set up camp on some unused land. The context was a weekend of activities organized to celebrate the Diggers, a group who had done the same thing on the same hill exactly 350 years before. As in that earlier time, this action attracted a good deal of concern in the area, and history was further repeated when, after beginning to plant out the area and establish themselves into a community, the latter-day Diggers were ejected from the hill.

It is likely that, until that point, few residents of that part of Surrey had heard of the Diggers. There was no plaque or monument to them in the vicinity, and little about the character of the area to suggest that establishing a memorial to a group sometimes known as 'England's first communists' would be the local council's priority. It is also not unlikely that some of the Diggers' modern counterparts had only the haziest knowledge about their seventeenth-century forebears or their leader and main theorist, Gerrard Winstanley. Certainly few would have had opportunity to study his writings. But that is not the point: what the Diggers once stood for, that people would never be truly free until the earth became once more a 'common treasury' for all to share, was once again being asserted and, indeed, enacted. Winstanley and his band may not have made it onto the pages of most standard works of politics, literature, history or religion, nor even been remembered in the area where they operated, but that was no reflection on the continuing relevance of their ideas. The insights they had had in their day were still inspiring people today, even if the social and political climate in 1999 was hardly more receptive to them than it was in 1649.

Winstanley is one of the people in this book, along with a host of his contemporaries who are also largely unknown and who might also be seen as history's losers. Some belonged to movements which have survived to the present day – through good organization, good discipline or perhaps an ability to keep their ambitions within the limits of the possible; others were involved with groups or sects whose hopes were more immediate and which, when dashed, disappeared as quickly as they arose. But all are of interest to us today, not just because we need to know what people did and said and thought and believed in the past, but because the issues which concerned them have concerned every generation since.

Some of the characters here are also 'larger than life', and for that reason alone their stories are worth telling. Among those we shall meet are Lodowicke Muggleton, for 40 years the leader of a movement which held him to be one of the Two Last Witnesses foretold in the Book of Revelation and which, almost as unbelievably, survived him by nearly three hundred years; Anna Trapnel, whose dying mother prayed that she would receive a double portion of blessing and who fasted for 12 days in a bed in Whitehall recounting prophecies and visions that made even Oliver Cromwell's government react; Abiezer Coppe, who with fellow Ranters abolished the concept of sin and lived accordingly while writing prose of a unique genre which continues to astound literary scholars today; James Nayler, who re-enacted the original Palm Sunday by riding a donkey into Bristol to the accompaniment of adoring women and was all but put to death for his trouble by a Parliament which spent six weeks deciding his fate; and a host of others from all strata of society, operating mainly outside the theatres of power, but trying to make sense of the events that they witnessed and imagining a better world which they not only believed to be possible but which they themselves could help to bring about.

෨๑

The years in our focus – roughly the mid-1640s to the Restoration of the monarchy in 1660 – have been described as the most traumatic and turbulent in English history. Whether their key events should be grouped together under the heading 'rebellion', 'revolution' or any other label continues to exercise historians, but what can be said is that the combined effect of three very bloody civil wars, the trial and execution of the Archbishop of Canterbury and the king, and the abolition of institutions such as the monarchy, House of Lords, Star Chamber, bishops and church courts combined to create a breakdown in censorship which allowed ideas hitherto considered heretical and kept underground to surface in print and in word.

It was not a complete free-for-all, of course: laws were still passed banning 'blasphemous and execrable' opinions on pain of death, and more than a few on our cast-list spent time in prison for publishing their views or had their books destroyed and meetings broken up. But the relative freedom of those years did allow a wide variety of religious, political and social views to circulate across society, such that, through the mass of printed material which has survived, we are able to gain a fascinating glimpse of what some people thought in those extraordinary times. Just how much freedom people thought they had to circulate their ideas in print once the landscape began to change can be seen from the fact that, while in 1640 just 22 tracts were printed, in 1642 the total was nearly 2,000. And the potential of these to subvert good order was not lost on those concerned to see it upheld, one writer noting in 1641 that the 'ink-squittering treacherous pamphlets' produced by sects operating outside of the established church 'are the main prop and pillar to uphold the sovereign unsavoury power of their factious conventicles'.

The phenomenon of the army becoming a political actor also played an important role in the spread of ideas. Formed in the mid-1640s to finish the job of defeating the king, and deliberately placed beyond the direct control of both the Lords and Commons, the New Model Army was, by the end of the decade, a major independent force, developing its own ideology, issuing public manifestoes and – as when Colonel Pride forcibly debarred from the House MPs committed to continuing discussions with the king –

not afraid to impose its will on Parliament. The Army was an important breeding ground for a range of political ideas, reformist and revolutionary, and a number of the people we shall meet would have debated and discussed these while serving in its ranks – most notably Levellers, who worked hard to get purchase for their programme among the troops, but also Baptists and future Fifth Monarchists, Quakers and others.

The role that religion played in people's thinking, and, indeed, in the shaping of the events of those two decades, cannot be overstated. While there were a host of economic, political and social factors contributing to the civil wars, it was religious issues that primarily drove the conflict – from Charles' attempts to impose the Prayer Book in Scotland, to a widespread fear of Catholicism, to the power of the bishops. As king and archbishop looked to make the church less Calvinist in its theology and more ritualistic in its practice, Puritans, fearing a return to 'popery' and wanting to keep the church 'reformed', joined forces to oppose him. Cromwell's conclusion that 'religion was not at first the thing contested for, but God brought it to that issue at last ... and at last it proved to be that which was most dear to us' is well known, and one of the most respected historians of the period, John Morrill, has suggested that the English civil war was 'the last of Europe's wars of religion'.[1] By the time the war was over the victorious party had proscribed all the 'monuments of superstition and idolatry' introduced by Archbishop Laud – such as altar rails, crucifixes, statues and images; outlawed the Book of Common Prayer and 39 Articles; abolished Christmas, Easter and Whitsuntide; and attempted to furnish the church with a Presbyterian, non-episcopal form of government.

That Anglicanism did not disappear is important to remember when considering the impact of the groups who *did* reject it; the majority of the faithful continued using the Prayer Book and taking communion at Easter and Christmas, and the cohesion of parish life was greatly valued. We shall meet laypeople as well as clergy who thought Quakers and Baptists should be hanged for their contempt for the doctrines accepted by the majority, and the potential of their preaching and practices to disrupt parochial unity. But also significant is the extent to which the ending of the state church's monopoly on religion led to the emergence of hundreds of new independent congregations and the growth of a culture of dissent which was to have a substantial impact on events both up to and beyond 1660. Even simple statistics can indicate the extent of this impact: the number of Baptist churches grew from a handful in the 1630s to 36 in London alone in 1646 to around 300 by 1660, with a total membership of perhaps 25,000; and, from a standing start at the beginning of the 1650s, Quakers numbered perhaps 60,000 by the end of the decade.

So we need to take religion into account when trying to understand the events of the time and the way people thought and acted: God was not indifferent to the affairs of his English flock. Both Parliament and the King regularly instituted national days of fasting, prayer and repentance, and there was a widespread sense that the unfolding drama had a wider, apocalyptic, significance. The debates between the Levellers and the army grandees at Putney had regular (sometimes five-hour) prayer breaks. Religion could both inspire change and legitimate the *status quo*, and it infused the thinking of all sides. Cromwell famously sought the mind of God before taking important decisions, and had no doubt that he was seeing God fulfilling 'those promises that he hath held forth of things to be accomplished in the later times'. His army, like its leader, was an agent of divine Providence. A 'Souldiers Pocket Bible' was produced to remind parliamentary troops that they had Scripture (and the Lord) on their side.

But Charles, too, had divine authority to engage in war, for God 'will not suffer rebels or traitors to prosper'. For a monarch who ruled by divine right, religion was a tool for keeping power, for, as he himself said, 'where was there ever obedience where religion did not teach it?' Like his forebears, Charles knew the people were 'governed by the pulpit more than the sword in time of peace' – that, as an anti-Quaker tract put it, 'if there was not a minister in every parish you would quickly find cause to increase the number of constables' – and relied on his university-schooled divines to explain the Scriptures to their flock. But since the Reformation the masses could consult and interpret Scripture themselves, and they might find that it sanctioned, in the words of Mary's song in Luke, the removal of the powerful from their thrones and the lifting up of the lowly and meek: indeed, if they read the Geneva version, which many did, they might find the subversive implications of various texts suggested in the margin. We know that Cromwell studied many Scriptures in the months leading up to the execution of Charles, among them chapters 6–8 of Judges, which relate to Gideon, the farmer called to shake up and lead the armies of Israel to overcome their foes and execute their kings.

The Bible played a major part in shaping thought. On one level people turned to Scripture in search of validation for their various positions: to persuade a sceptic or convince an opponent one needed chapter and verse to back up the view being proposed. Even the Levellers, who argued their case strongly on the grounds of reason and natural law, used the Bible for support. Knowledge of the Bible was so widespread that a preacher or writer need only refer to the name of a character or incident to make their point – which, as Christopher Hill points out, could be of particular advantage when their purpose was 'to remind [their] audience of parts of the story which [they] did not think it prudent to empha-size'![2] But in an age in which 'politics' and 'religion' were not the focus of separate debates, the Bible also provided not just the grammar in which to frame ideas, but a source for those ideas as well. Thus the Leveller leader John Lilburne uses the language of Genesis to argue for political equality and condemn tyranny, but also grounds his thinking in the creation narrative. And Gerrard Winstanley's interpretation of the 'fall' as the introduction of the practice of buying and selling the land finds him couching his pro-gramme to bring the earth back into common ownership in terms of the struggle between 'flesh' and 'spirit', Adam and Christ, within both the individual and society. When Levellers, Fifth Monarchists, Diggers and others spoke of the Civil War as 'England's Exodus' and Cromwell as the 'new Moses', they saw it both as a metaphor for their experience, and themselves also, like the Israelites of old, under the delivering hand of God. 'Crucially', as John Coffey argues, 'this was a story that could capture the imagination and put fire in the belly'.[3]

In the Puritan milieu of the 1640s the Bible was the final court of appeal. Debates among the Baptists centred on a correct understanding of what the Bible said about church order; Quakers were pressed to explain how their 'Christ within' was also the historical figure of the gospels; Winstanley was challenged by his most trenchant opponent to justify his digging on common land from Scripture. Of course, appeal to the Bible allowed anyone to claim divine sanction for their views, a reason why kings in the past had prevented its circulation and imposed a uniformity of beliefs through a national church. But in the 1640s and 50s, with the power of the established church on the wane, authority was up for grabs, and a succession of prophets and preachers began to emerge claiming direct inspiration from God and a warrant to disclose his mind and will. The crudest example would be Muggleton and his cousin John Reeve, who were accorded power from on high to damn any who did not accept their authority as the Two Last Witnesses, and who both exercised it freely; but perhaps it is only as we recognize the extent to which people believed God still spoke directly to women and men that we can understand the respect accorded to a visionary such as Anna Trapnel, and the seriousness with which her utterances were received, or the threat implicit in a 'thus saith the Lord' on the lips of the Ranter Abiezer Coppe.

The influence of the Bible in these years is particularly evident in the case of its prophetic texts. Two books in particular, Daniel in the Old Testament and Revelation in the New, were understood to describe figuratively the denouement of history, and amid the tumult of the 1640s and 50s people read them with particular interest. Many who fought for Parliament had been encouraged to see the war against the king in apocalyptic terms – the struggle between Christ and Antichrist – and few would not have shared Milton's supposition that Christ was 'the eternal and shortly-expected King' who would 'open the clouds to judge the several kingdoms of this world'. Decoding the images in the apocalyptic texts – the beast with ten horns, the 42 months, Antichrist itself – was important for discerning the drift of events, though a conviction that history was moving toward the millennium, the thousand-year rule of the saints, which the saints themselves might play a role in bringing in, could prove deeply subversive. Only the Fifth Monarchists, who saw in the execution of Charles the downfall of the fourth great kingdom depicted by Daniel and the stage being set for the fifth, actually built a political movement around their beliefs, but a sense that Christ would presently come to reign through, with or even within his saints, informed most of the sects and movements in the years following the Civil War.

The fascination of the 1640s and 50s lies not in the novelty of the beliefs and ideas which flourished but in the fact that there was freedom at that time to express them openly. Few of the ideas we shall meet were original, even if those canvassing them would claim to have received them through direct inspiration from God or engagement with the Bible rather than a study of history or earlier writers. Millenarianism, for example, was a creed of the earliest Christians, whose anticipation of the reign of Christ on earth looked so subversive to church leaders with a stake in the here-and-now that they made it a heresy in the fifth century. We find it surfacing again in the twelfth century with Joachim of Fiore, and on the fringes of the European Reformation – including, most famously (though untypically), in the attempt by extreme Anabaptists in the 1530s to take the city of Münster by force and turn it into the New Jerusalem.

Some of the ideas propounded by Ranters and Quakers – that heaven and hell are in this world; that the Spirit within has precedence over the Word without; that the Bible should be read as allegory – were held earlier by the Family of Love, and had reached England from the continent by the 1570s. Like the Diggers, Familists held their property in common, a position also championed by John Ball from the 1360s (not to mention the Jerusalem church in Acts chapter 4). Lollards shared many of the anti-clerical sentiments of the Quakers, Levellers and others 200 years earlier, and Grindletonians and Seekers held heretical views a decade or two before the Ranters. The practice of separating from the national church may not have been unknown in the 1530s, and was certainly being advocated in Elizabethan times by the followers of Robert Browne and Henry Barrow. There were Anabaptists in England until 1575, and independent Baptist churches from 1612.

This is not to argue that a subterranean 'golden thread' of subversive and heretical views can be traced through English history (though the case has been argued by some historians of the left, and research has suggested that there may be areas of the country where such views were handed on); but it is to observe that the ideas we encounter between 1640 and 1660 were not formed in a vacuum, even if the groups that emerged then took them to greater extremes as a consequence of the extra freedom they enjoyed to operate.

ৡক্৵

If the focus in this book is on people who joined together around a certain body of ideas, the temptation should be avoided to see the sects or movements of the 1640s and 50s as discrete, easily identifiable bodies. While Baptist churches came to insist on believers' baptism as a pre-requisite for membership, and worked hard to build 'associations' of local churches, no group had any centralized structure or formal membership such as we expect of organizations today. Even the Levellers, who in some ways prefigure modern-day political parties, were not a united, disciplined body promoting a commonly agreed agenda. It would thus be misleading to adopt too readily nouns such as 'Quakerism' or 'Ranterism', perhaps even to speak of what Ranters or Levellers collectively 'thought', especially since our sources will generally be limited to the writings and speeches of their leaders. As Jonathan Scott has pointed out, if we use 'Levellerism' at all it is the sense that we understand it as an 'activity' – petitioning, publishing, agitating and so on – rather than an ideology.[4]

An indication of the fluidity of these groups is the ease with which people moved from one to another. The Digger leader Winstanley, for example, may have been a Baptist in his youth and appears to have died as a Quaker, and the Leveller leader John Lilburne also became a Friend. A number of Baptists became Fifth Monarchists and Quakers in the 1650s, and Lawrence Clarkson appears to have been successively a Presbyterian, an Independent (a forerunner of the Congregationalists), a Baptist, a Seeker, a Ranter and a Muggletonian! Samuel Fisher, whom we shall meet as a Baptist, had earlier undergone Presbyterian ordination and was later to become a Quaker.

Our focus on 'movements' necessarily precludes discussion of individuals who may have shared some of their convictions and beliefs but did not identify with them, of whom the two most obvious examples are perhaps John Bunyan and John Milton. Bunyan had strong links with the Baptists, and appears from his writings to have shared many of the social and political attitudes of the movements of the day, if not their theology; and, like many Baptists and others, he would also have been exposed to a variety of political views while serving in the Parliamentary army. Yet apart from a cryptic remark in one of his late writings – 'I did use to be much taken with one sect of Christians, for that it was usually their way, when they made mention of the name of Jesus to call him the blessed King of glory' – we have no evidence that he sought affiliation with any movement or group, aside from his local church.[5] Milton also eschewed identification with the political movements of his day, though he was a passionate apologist for non-conformity and, as author of works such as *Eikonoklastes* and *The Tenure of Kings and Magistrates*, an even more eloquent and powerful advocate of the Commonwealth. Christopher Hill detects in Milton ideas which later came to be associated with Ranters, and has also pointed to a remarkable similarity between his beliefs and those of John Reeve.[6]

One problem we encounter in studying the groups of the 1640s and 50s is the respective weight to give to their own claims for what they believed and did and those of their detractors. This is especially true of the Ranters, whose extreme unconventionality attracted ridicule and opprobrium in equal measure. So many of the accounts of the Ranters' behaviour overlap that it is possible to construct a general picture of who they were – but is it a picture of a phenomenon which actually 'existed', or were 'Ranters', rather like witches, an invention of their contemporaries who needed an 'image' on which to project all their fears of social and religious deviance? Even the writings of those we might usefully identify as Ranters are of limited help, because in the case of, for example, Abiezer Coppe, his work is so multi-layered and his tone often ironic.

Quakers, Baptists and Diggers were also often attacked in print and their beliefs and practices mocked and distorted. Baptists were forever disavowing the connection their opponents so readily made between themselves and the Münster Anabaptists, and we need to remember also that even the names by which many movements became known were inventions of their foes, including 'Quakers', 'Levellers' and 'Diggers'. The 'Digger' leader Winstanley much pre-ferred the term 'True Leveller', which conveyed his intent to see the earth made once again 'a common treasury', while the 'Levellers' themselves frequently denied that they had intent to level out prop-erty and might sign off their tracts 'The Levellers (Falsely so called)'.

A very fertile – though contentious – source of knowledge of some of the religious views which flourished in the 1640s is Thomas Edwards' *Gangraena*, a massive, three-volume work cata-loguing 'the errors, heresies, blasphemies, and insolent proceedings of the sectaries of these times'. We shall meet Edwards and his book often in these pages. A passionate advocate of a compulsory national church along Presbyterian lines, Edwards was appalled by the concept of 'toleration', and lambasted all who claimed the right to worship in their own way and under their own lights (not least Baptists). Edwards takes care to document his cases and, as a lead-ing scholar of his work, Ann Hughes, has said, 'there is little sign that [he] invented his material, and many of his details of name, time, and place can be confirmed from other sources'.[7] Yet the polemical intent of his writing should warn us to approach it with some caution, and, as Hughes has argued, it is less interesting to ask questions about its plausibility than about what it might tell us of the age in which it was written. Certainly Edwards' contemporaries were divided as to the value of his work, some seeing him as a 'faithful friend of truth', others as a forger or liar. Milton famously attacked him in verse, and one of his (disappointed) readers felt he could only justify the huge price he had paid for his copy by using it 'piecemeal in the house of office'!

Edwards describes the people he deplored as 'illiterate Mechanick persons' who saw no need of learning or books, yet more than a few Levellers, Ranters and others attended university or grammar school, and many others who enjoyed little formal education wrote prose of extraordinary clarity, power and insight. 'Mechanic' implies manual worker or artisan, yet many sectaries were of considerably higher social status and even minor gentry. As Nicholas McDowell has pointed out, research into the social composition of separatist congregations and movements such as the Fifth Monarchists and Quakers indicates that the rank-and-file membership came not from the bottom 50 per cent of the population – labourers, cottagers, paupers – but from the 'middle' sort of people, 'independent craftsmen and small tradesmen … husbandmen and yeomen'. The only exception is the small groups of labourers who constituted the Diggers, though even that generalization could well be contested.[8]

Women played a significant role in many of the groups, even if this was often hidden. In society they were regarded as naturally inferior to men – 'not endowed with like strength and constancy of mind', as the Homily to Marriage put it – so when the House of Commons told the Leveller women petitioners 'to go home, and look after your own business, and meddle with your housewifery' because an answer had already been given to their husbands, it was not saying anything unusual. Yet among Baptists, Quakers, Fifth Monarchists and other groups, while conventional attitudes may have generally prevailed, a recognition that God might use extraordinary means in extraordinary times to convey his mind gave remarkable authority to those women perceived to be endowed with divine grace.

In fact, given the lowly and despised status of women in society, there was a perception that they were actually closer to God and therefore more likely to be chosen by God to speak (and did not St Paul affirm that it was God's intent to use the 'base things' of the world to confound the wise?). A passage in the Old Testament book of Joel (and found also in the Acts of the Apostles) foretelling that in the last days sons and daughters will prophesy and God's spirit will fall upon 'handmaids' was widely read, even if other churches felt happier with Paul's instruction to the Corinthians that women not be permitted to speak in church. The growth of the Quakers owed much to the peculiar gifts of Margaret Fell, and propagandists and preachers such as Elizabeth Fletcher and Elizabeth Leavens, and as a movement it was particularly adept at recognizing and channelling the gifts that a woman might have in the area of ecstatic prophecy, preaching and evangelism, and as a spouse, mother, correspondent and sick-visitor. Despite the chauvinistic tendencies of its figurehead, the Muggletonians appointed women to positions of leadership and received those joining up independently of their husbands.

An interesting philosophical question could be asked about the rationale for selecting the groups included here. It is true that they share a broad core of concerns – not least a rejection of an established church maintained by the tithe and a wish for toleration and freedom of conscience – and that they generally seek to push matters farther than the various parliaments, and Cromwell himself, seem prepared to go in the 1650s. But they also represent a wide range of theological, not to say eschatological, positions, and differ vastly in terms of their aims and visions, and their attitudes to politics and morality. At one time the thread connecting them would have been their 'radicalism', a term which was often not precisely defined but which it was assumed did convey the impression that these were groups who wanted much deeper political, economic, social and religious change than was actually happening, if not the overthrow of the *status quo* to create the possibility of building something new.

In one sense the term is a useful shorthand, and it has been used in almost every study of the Civil War and Interregnum sects since Christopher Hill's seminal 1972 study *The World Turned Upside Down* – subtitled 'radical ideas during the English revolution'. In recent years, however, the case for abandoning the word in a seventeenth-century context has been made with some force, both on the grounds that its use is anachronistic – the sense in which it is generally used today, to describe someone seeking extreme change or innovation, is of eighteenth-century origin – and because, as Conal Condren has argued, what people struggled to prove in the seventeenth century was not the originality or newness of their ideas but the extent to which they were rooted in tradition and committed to its preservation. Discourse in that century, as Condren puts it, 'was less structured in terms of radicals versus conservatives than in terms of alternative claimants of the mantle of authentic tradition and its necessary conservation.'[9] Or as Tim Cooper says, those whom we have always termed radicals 'may simply be those who were least effective in employing seventeenth-century polemical strategies that aggressively sought to claim the mantle of conservatism and paint opponents as innovators.'[10] Glenn Burgess has also made the point that, if 'radical' is a political category, it hardly makes sense to apply it to groups whose understanding of how change occurs allowed no room for political action – by which he means, with the exception of the Levellers, every group here. It is not that these so-called 'radicals' could not envisage dramatic change or did not believe that the world should be turned upside down, Burgess argues, they just did not see human action as having a part.[11]

As its title implies, the purpose of this book is not to take on that debate, though it is not uninformed by it. In seeking simply to introduce the main characters, ideas and endeavours of the various movements I have adopted the general framework used by previous studies, without seeking to debate its merits or weaknesses. In the wake of revisionist and now post-revisionist approaches to seventeenth-century studies it is clearly time for the criteria by which we talk of 'radicals' – if we talk about them in those terms at all – to be reappraised, but it is not my intent to discuss that here.

Yet, having said this, there is something about the term 'radical' which is exciting and edgy and which still impels me to use it without apology. We need a catch-all word to conjure up that spirit of challenging accepted wisdom and practice, imagining and promoting a better world and being committed to active engagement to bring it about; and while not all of the groups here did all of these things all of the time, describing them collectively as 'radical' still strikes me as saying something meaningful about them to the contemporary reader. As Edward Vallance – who wrestled with this question in a book on 'radical history' published in 2009 – says, we should not too readily abandon the idea of a 'British "radical tradition"' in the face of conservative opposition; and even if, in so doing, we do not want to go so far as to argue for 'a historical continuum in which the baton of popular struggle was passed from one group to the next', holding to a 'good commonsense definition' of the term can enable us to recognize those who, in their own time, 'advocated the transformation of the existing *status quo* rather than merely reforming it to ameliorate its worst aspects.'[12] Christopher Hill once confessed that he did not know 'how otherwise than as radicals to describe people who in the mid-seventeenth century (and earlier) held unorthodox views on religion and politics which set them beyond the pale of the respectable groups which we shall call Anglicans, Presbyterians or Independents', and I'm inclined to share his view that, until somebody comes up with a better word to describe them, we should continue to call them by that name![13]

The modest aim of this book means that I have not attempted to engage here with the vast scholarship the 'radicals' have generated of late. Since the early 1970s, scholars in the fields of literature, politics, history, women's studies, theology and more besides have produced a mass of books, articles and papers on these groups, exploring their beliefs, writings, impact and inter-relationship from a wide range of angles. In one sense this is not surprising and is indeed welcome – there is a deep mine of material here, of which we have only barely begun to make sense – but a general survey such as this cannot hope to do justice to all the scholarship it has attracted. Which is not to say that I have not reflected the most recent work with respect to each movement in what I have written: I have certainly sought to do that. But where an issue might be strongly debated – such as whom the Levellers actually thought should be enfranchised, or the extent to which we can meaningfully talk of an entity called 'Ranters' – I have tried simply to summarize the different sides rather than offer a firm opinion.

Above all, my rule of thumb has been to let our subjects speak for themselves, rather than venture an opinion as to what they might have 'actually meant'. The most valuable legacy that many of the people discussed in this book have left us is their prose, and it would be a travesty merely to write about Coppe's rhetorical flourishes, Overton's passionate advocacy, Trapnel's inspirational visions, even Muggleton's vituperative cursings, without allowing us to read them for ourselves. That so much of their work is not always in print and difficult to track down, even in this age of on-line resources, is another reason why opportunity has been made to engage with them directly here.

'The old world ... is running up like parchment in fire, and wearing away', wrote Gerrard Winstanley in April 1649, three months after the execution of the King; and many sensed with him that profound changes were afoot, that God was shaking the foundations, that the world just might be about to be 'turned upside down'. That the turmoil of the 1640s did not produce the transformation many people anticipated makes the story of how they made sense of the hopes, possibilities and disappointments of the period no less fascinating.

CHAPTER ONE

Baptists

BAPTISTS ARE ONE of the few dissenting movements which flourished during the civil war years to have survived to the present day. Now very much a mainstream 'free' church, they are chiefly characterized by a non-liturgical form of worship with a strong emphasis on preaching, and a conviction that baptism – usually by full immersion in water – is to be administered only to people consciously professing faith, and not, therefore, to infants. In adhering to these practices they demonstrate a historical continuity with their forebears in the seventeenth century; but while today Baptist beliefs and practices are hardly likely to provoke social unrest – indeed, in the USA, the term 'Baptist' is almost a synonym for political conservatism – the movement's founders were regularly denounced as heretical and subversive, a threat to good order and the stability of both church and state.

In the sixteenth and seventeenth centuries the terms 'Baptist' and 'Anabaptist' were bandied about in much the same way as 'Communist' was in the USA in the 1950s. In 1646 the influential Scottish divine Robert Baillie published a tract describing 'Anabaptism' as 'the true fountain' of what he believed to be all the heretical groups then in evidence, 'and most of the other errors which for the time do trouble the Church of England'. For Baillie, these believers were a danger to 'the whole fabric of our churches and kingdoms', and he was not alone in his concerns about this small but fiercely independent movement.

It was the ready association their detractors made with the continental Anabaptists of the previous century that made life hard for the early Baptists in England. It was not just that 'Anabaptism' had become a byword for subversion, on account of its adherents' strong insistence that true believers should separate entirely from the world and reject all civil governments and a state church; its reputation had been tarnished by a notorious episode in 1534 when an extreme tendency of the movement, foregoing their principles of pacifism and separatism, took control of the city of Münster and tried to establish, by force, the 'new Jerusalem' founded on proto-communist principles. Inspired by the charismatic Jan Bockelson (John of Leiden), the group survived a siege of the city by local princes for over a year until they were finally overcome and put to the sword. Even a hundred years later simply the evocation of the term 'Münster' was enough to send shivers down the spines of good upright people in England, and the Baptists' detractors used it to good effect. As a preacher at St Bartholomew in the City opined in 1632, 'then are the Anabaptists mad, who would reject all law, and make the whole world level; denying obedience to laws and lawful magistrates, a disease begun in the distempered heads of John of Leiden, and the mad men of Münster, opposed by the holy zeal of Luther, whose doctrine of reformation was dangerously mistaken by those fanatics.'

Thus the great scourge of all heretics in the 1640s, Thomas Edwards, after a diatribe against the 'errors, blasphemies and practices of the sectaries' in his infamous volume *Gangraena*, spoke of England having become 'already in many places a chaos, a Babel, another Amsterdam, yea, worse; we are beyond that, and in the highway to Münster'. A few years earlier a tract had appeared with a similar sentiment in its title: *A Warning for England especially for London in the Famous History of the Frantick Anabaptists*. In the 1650s, a pamphlet issued by the government to justify a disturbance caused by some soldiers at the funeral of a Baptist pastor in a small Oxfordshire town bore the title 'Münster and Abingdon'! Perhaps, as J. F. McGregor has put it, in the fevered atmosphere generated by 'the emergence of popular agitation supporting the parliamentary cause ... the fear that London might become another

Münster did not seem too fanciful',[1] but it exposed the Baptists to more hostility and suspicion than they perhaps warranted. It is easy to understand the frustration of Leveller leader Richard Overton, himself a Baptist, when, in 1646, he wondered, 'Who writ the history of the Anabaptists but their enemies?'

The irony was that the English Baptists of the seventeenth century neither accepted the label 'Anabaptist' nor had their roots in that tradition. Their reason for eschewing the term 'Anabaptist' was straightforward: it meant, after all, re-baptizer, and Baptists held that when they baptized believers they were not administering a second baptism but a first, the ritual performed on infants being no baptism at all. The term was thus at best misleading and at worst downright offensive, and, until their nomenclature became more widely respected, they preferred themselves to be described in terms such as 'the group of baptized believers meeting at...'. To what extent their lineage might be traced back to the continental Anabaptists of the previous century has been a matter of scholarly debate for some years, but the consensus view now is that the links made at the time by their opponents were a result of wishful thinking and not historically grounded. As respected Baptist historian B. R. White wrote in 1996, even the most 'careful studies ... seeking to estimate the influence of Anabaptism upon both General and Calvinistic Baptist origins found no significant influence could be decisively proved'.[2]

Those who have argued that the roots of the English Baptist tradition do lie in the soil of continental Anabaptism place great emphasis on the fact that the first of its churches was formed in Holland. Thus Mervyn Himbury in his *British Baptists: A Short History* suggests that it is not without significance that the group of English separatists who first openly formed themselves into what we would now recognize as a Baptist church only did so once they had left these shores (to escape persecution) and 'settled in a country (Holland) where the baptizers' movement (Anabaptist) had been active for more than seventy years'.[3] But what is interesting is that the leader of that fellowship, the former Anglican clergyman John Smyth, deliberately distanced himself from the Dutch Anabaptists, choosing to baptize himself – once he had come to the view that baptism should be for believers only – rather than request them to baptize him. Indeed, he explicitly stated at that time that 'that there was no church to whom we [his group of English exiles] could join with a good conscience to have baptism from them.'

That Smyth took this decision consciously, rather than in igno-rance of the existence of a Mennonite community in Holland, has been persuasively argued by Stephen Wright, who cites evidence of Smyth's group having contact with local Mennonites (or Waterlanders) but disagreeing with them on certain doctrinal ques-tions.[4] Smyth's decision not to request a Mennonite baptism did not, however, prevent his critics identifying his act of self-baptism (sometimes known as 'se-baptism') as 'Anabaptist', one, Henry Ainsworth, noting that 'Mr Smyth anabaptised himself with water, he and his followers having dischurched themselves and dissolved their communion; yet he in that state, preached, and anabaptised himself and then anabaptised others.' Ainsworth also linked Smyth's 'Anabaptism' with the influence of 'the Devil'.

It is also clear that Smyth's church could not have drawn upon any English Anabaptist tradition, there being no Anabaptist com-munities in England in the decades leading up to Smyth's decamp-ment to Holland in 1608. While Anabaptist ideas probably reached England from the continent during the reigns of Henry VIII, Edward VI and Mary, there is little evidence to suggest that they were adopted by native English people, and none to suggest that Anabaptist congregations existed in England during the last quarter of the sixteenth century. The last Anabaptist group of that century for which any records exist was disbanded in 1575, some of its con-gregation – all of whom were Dutch – being executed.

Whatever their detractors may have said, the first English Baptists were inheritors, not of any Anabaptist tradition, but of the puritan and separatist movements within their native country. The English separatist movement, associated particularly with Robert Browne and often referred to as 'Brownist', originated just as Anabaptism disappeared, and there is no evidence that the one

4

influenced the other or that the movements had common origins. Certainly in the case of Smyth, he spent the years immediately before his exile struggling to survive as a member of the church into which he had been ordained, and saw his own difficulties, and his decision finally to separate from the church, within the context of an ongoing tension between the Archbishop of Canterbury and that minority of clergy which refused to conform.

Before Smyth died in 1612 he had second thoughts about the validity of the baptism he had administered to himself and his flock, and decided to seek membership with the Waterlanders he had originally shunned. This, perhaps, involved yet another baptism. Smyth's adoption of a view of salvation more akin to the Mennonites' own Arminian beliefs might also have precipitated this move. But not all Smyth's members shared his disquiet about their baptisms, and, following a split, a group under the leadership of Nottinghamshire gentleman Thomas Helwys returned home to set up the first Baptist church on English soil in Spitalfields, London, in 1612. Helwys was deeply upset by Smyth's decision to seek union with the Waterlanders, and rejected their claim that only their baptism was valid and that only they could ordain elders. Although a layman, Helwys excommunicated Smyth and those who supported him, returning home with a small fraction of the congregation.

Helwys had already seen his considerable estate at Broxtowe confiscated by the Crown during his exile, but he immediately signalled his intent not to lie low by writing to James I to request him to tolerate his and others' separatist beliefs. This appeal was sent with a copy of a tract entitled *A Short Declaration of the Mistery of Iniquity*, and in it Helwys resisted any attempt to win over the king by flattery, reminding him bluntly that he was 'a mortal man, and not God, therefore hath no power over the immortal souls of his subjects'. Helwys acknowledged that, by returning to England, he and his followers risked persecution: indeed, they had come 'to lay down their lives in their own country for Christ and his truth'.

Helwys' tone in this tract should not hide the fact that he was deeply patriotic, believing that all the king's subjects should pay allegiance to his majesty's person, crown and dignity. His real bugbear was the bishops of the church and their tendency to arrogate to themselves powers that rightly belonged to the civil magistrate. In fact, Helwys' respect for magistrates (which was rooted perhaps in his own training as a lawyer) was matched only by his loathing of their ecclesiastical counterparts, and he even went so far as to suggest that the king do away with all bishops, confiscate their lands and wealth, and thereby save himself the trouble of collecting taxes!

Together with his colleague John Murton, who returned to England with him, Helwys spent time in Newgate prison, possibly dying there in 1616. Other Baptist leaders also appear to have been interned in those early years. Archbishop Bancroft's commitment to enforcing subscription to the church and its articles made life difficult for all dissenting groups, and during the 25 years following Helwys' death his followers were forced to endure a somewhat perilous, underground existence in their native England. Yet the movement grew and spread, such that by 1626 there were congregations as far afield as Tiverton in Devon, Sarum in Wiltshire, Lincoln and Coventry as well as London, with a total membership of around 150 souls.

Something of the flavour of Baptist worship in the earliest days may be gleaned from a letter written by two members of John Smyth's church in Amsterdam, Anne and Hugh Bromhead, in 1609. The letter is a reply to one from a contact in London dated 13 July, so it describes the church subsequent to Smyth's 're-baptisms'.

The order of the worship and government of our church is:

1. We begin with a prayer, after read some one or two chapters of the Bible, give the sense thereof and confer upon the same; that done, we lay aside our books and after a solemn prayer made by the first speaker he

> *propoundeth some text out of the scripture and*
> *prophesieth out of the same by the space of one hour or*
> *three quarters of an hour. After him standeth up a second*
> *speaker and prophesieth out of the said text the like time*
> *and space, sometimes more, sometimes less. After him,*
> *the third, the fourth, the fifth etc, as the time will give*
> *leave. Then the first speaker concludeth with prayer as he*
> *began with prayer, with an exhortation to contribution to*
> *the poor, which collection being made is also concluded*
> *with prayer. This morning exercise begins at eight of the*
> *clock and continueth unto twelve of the clock. The like*
> *course of exercise is observed in the afternoon from two*
> *of the clock to five or six of the clock. Last of all the*
> *execution of the government of the Church is handled.*

Apart from the length of the services – four hours in the morning and between three and four hours in the afternoon – and the apparent lack of singing or any variation from the pattern of reading, prayer and exposition, two features stand out, both of which demonstrate the radical hue of these meetings. First, the preaching is conducted not by a learned, university-educated divine, but by ordinary members who appear not to have any special status (either from each other or from the congregation as a whole). One speaker – perhaps the first – may have been the pastor, John Smyth, but, if so, the Bromheads did not think that significant enough to mention. And second, sermons with a reliance upon book-learning and scholarship are clearly eschewed in favour of allowing the Spirit to speak through the preacher: books must be 'laid aside', not only so that any temptation to obfuscate the plain meaning of the text by indulging in sophisticated scriptural interpretation is avoided, but so that the preacher's experience rather than his or her erudition takes precedence. Several decades later this emphasis was still strong in Baptist circles, the Calvinistic Baptist leader William Kiffin recording in the 1630s that his group spent time together 'in prayer, and in communicating to each other what experience we had received from the Lord' and subsequently 'read some portion of Scripture, and spake from it what it pleased God to enable us'. John Bunyan records in his *Grace Abounding to the Chief of Sinners* that he 'preached what he did feel, what he smartingly did feel'.

In an echo of the Bromheads' comments Helwys himself once remarked that 'all books, even the originals themselves, must be laid aside in the time of spiritual worship'. Like his fellow Baptists, Helwys was clear that the ordinary believer had no need of a learned priest in order to enjoy a knowledge of God: 'the most simplest soul that seeks the truth in sincerity may attain unto the knowledge of salvation contained in the Word of God', he declared. It was therefore not an issue for Baptists that Helwys, a layperson, should lead and pioneer a church, nor that unordained members of the congregation should preach and baptize.

While Baptists shared a conviction that the true, visible church of Christ comprised 'intentional' gathered congregations of baptized believers, a range of views over issues relating to church organization and points of doctrine existed from the earliest days. Among the group which returned from Amsterdam in 1609, for example, were some who found Helwys' anti-clericalism too extreme, and opinions also varied within the group as to who had the right to administer baptism and whether believers should be pacifists. The issue of 'separation' was also interpreted in different ways, and while a number of Baptist leaders defined the Church of England as a 'false church' and required their congregations to remain absolutely apart from it, other Baptist groups continued to meet with those who shared their Puritan convictions but had chosen to stay within the church's ranks. One such was a Calvinist congregation founded by Henry Jacob, who had returned from exile on the continent to found a church in London in 1616. Jacob had in fact signalled his position as early as 1605 when he wrote to the king expressing a wish to meet for worship outside the jurisdiction of the bishops, while also promising to 'keep brotherly communion with the rest of our English churches as they are now established'.

By the middle of the seventeenth century two separate movements were apparent within the English Baptist churches: the 'General' or

'Arminian Baptists', who took their steer from the Dutch theologian Jacobus Arminius, and who believed that Christ had died generally for all people; and the 'Particular' or 'Calvinistic Baptists', who held that Christ came to save a particular body of souls, the 'elect'. While the General Baptists could trace their roots back to the exiled church of Smyth and Helwys in Amsterdam, the Particular Baptists emerged in the 1630s from among the independent congregations in London, some of which had links to Jacob, becoming self-consciously a distinct grouping with the publication of a *Confession*, signed by their seven churches, in 1644. However, the temptation to see this division within the Baptists in clear-cut terms should be avoided: not all churches within one movement necessarily agreed on, for example, whether baptism should be administered to infants, and there was some transfer of churches and leaders between the two movements, particularly from the General Baptist side to the Particulars. One might also find General Baptists going into print in defence of particular redemption.

While the two movements agreed on many cardinal doctrines, there appears to have been a degree of rivalry between them, or at least between certain of their members. Hanserd Knollys, a former Anglican clergyman who had been instrumental in forming a Calvinistic Baptist church, was particularly outspoken in his condemnation of General Baptists: 'notwithstanding all this profession of general redemption, they themselves are the servants of corruptions' he wrote in the 1640s. Knollys was also noted for his preaching 'with all fierceness' against those of whom he disapproved. An Arminian critique of Calvinism, albeit rather more moderate in tone, appeared in *The Fountain of Free Grace Opened*, a statement of General Baptist beliefs published in 1645. A further source of tension between the two tendencies was the requirement by some General Baptists that any Particular brethren and sisters switching allegiance to their side be re-baptized, since their first baptism, into 'the wrong faith', was held to be invalid.

One matter on which Baptists did agree was that the rite of entry into the church should be baptism. For the General Baptists and most Calvinistic Baptists this meant *believers'* baptism, which they understood to have meaning, not in the sense that it 'conveyed' faith, but as an outward testimony or sign of a faith already held. It was, as a Particular Baptist document put it, a 'visible way of profession by which [believers] are distinguished from the world'. Some of the more vociferous of those who supported believers' baptism – including Kiffin and Knollys – considered those who practised infant baptism guilty of the sin of adding to Scripture, there being no text in either testament commanding the baptism of infants. Those of a different persuasion, however, pointed to parallels with circumcision in the Old Testament and wondered if an emphasis on believers, usually assumed to be 'adults', implied an indifference towards the spiritual wellbeing of children.

The key issue for Kiffin, Knollys and other Baptists was that only what was explicitly commanded in Scripture should become church practice: creating extra rules, which is what they understood paedo-baptists to be doing, was to undervalue the 'kingly office of Christ, in giving laws to his church'. John Smyth himself had been clear that 'infants are not to be baptized ... because there is neither precept nor example in the New Testament ... only they that did confess their sins, and confess their faith were baptized'. The issue of whether the Bible provided the only source for divine wisdom, which most Baptists in the seventeenth century professed to hold, was at the root of a number of their disputes with other groups.

The seriousness with which the issue of infant versus believers' baptism was taken can be gauged from the fact that both sides felt their very lives to be at risk on account of their respective stances. John Spilsbury, a leader of the Calvinistic Baptists in London (and founder of what was probably the first Particular Baptist church in England in 1638), noted in his robust defence of baptism by immersion, *A Treatise Concerning the Lawfull Subject of Baptisme*, that 'men [are] so incensed against me, as to seek my life, as some have done'. On the other hand, a debate between, on the one side, Knollys, Kiffin and another Calvinistic Baptist, Benjamin Cox, and the main spokesperson for the infant cause, the Presbyterian divine Edmund Calamy, had to be cancelled when rumours spread that the three Calvinists planned to bring 'swords, clubs and staves' to ensure that their view prevailed, and that Calamy would be fortunate to leave the proceedings alive! Interestingly, mention of the threat of violence appeared only in Calamy's report of the non-debate, not the Baptists'!

While most General Baptist churches were consistent in allowing no one to join their churches unless they had been baptized as believers, some Calvinistic churches did admit into membership those who had only been baptized as infants. These tended to be congregations which had originally been Independent (as Congregationalists were originally known) and practised both believers' and infant baptism. Many of the Calvinistic churches which operated a closed, baptized-believers-only, membership policy also practised what became known as 'closed communion', allowing only those baptized as believers to share in the Lord's Supper. An appendix to the Particular Baptist *Confession* of 1644, which had affirmed that baptism was to be 'dispensed only upon persons professing faith', made it clear that those churches who practise such baptism 'therefore do not admit any in the use of the supper, nor communicate with any in the use of this ordinance, but disciples baptized'.

A number of churches also adopted the practice of 'laying hands' upon baptized members, a tradition common among Dutch Anabaptists and linked with reception of the Holy Spirit. Thomas Edwards noted it being practised in 1645 in the church pastored by Edward Barber, which met near Threadneedle Street in the City, and the same year some of the congregation at the influential church led by Thomas Lambe at Bell Alley, Coleman Street, followed suit. At Bell Alley, however, the issue led to a major disagreement and split which resulted in Lambe, who steadfastly opposed the practice of the laying on of hands, becoming increasingly isolated from his fellow General Baptists as it became adopted more widely in their churches. In Barber's church the practice was used to commission members to 'preach into the countries, yea into the streets openly and publicly, yea to the doors of the Parliament House'.

By the 1640s both Particular and General Baptists were agreed that baptism must be by total immersion, symbolizing an identity with Christ in his death and resurrection: passing through the waters of baptism the believer 'died to sin' and then 'rose again' to begin a new life. Leading General Baptists such as Thomas Lambe and Edward Barber were known to be practising believers' baptism by immersion by 1641, and the 1644 Particular Baptist *Confession* is explicit in stressing that immersion meant 'dipping or plunging the whole body under water' as a sign of 'washing the whole soul in the blood of Christ'. 'As certainly as the body is buried under water and riseth again, so certainly shall the bodies of the saints be raised by the power of Christ, in the day of resurrection, to rise with Christ.' Henry Jessey, third pastor of the church founded by Henry Jacob and known as the Jacob-Lathrop-Jessey church after its first three leaders, thought immersion the right mode of baptism for infants.

The Baptists' practice of baptising by immersion did little to allay the fears of their critics who thought they were Anabaptists reincarnate, and the more so when, for fear of discovery, they conducted their baptisms at night in any nearby stream, pond or river. Reports that they were indulging in all manner of immoral and depraved activities – of the type once supposedly enjoyed by their spiritual forebears at Münster – circulated widely, and Baptist ministers not infrequently had to defend themselves in court against accusations of dipping women naked at night or lying with them in the water. A charge sheet against the General Baptist, Samuel Oates, in 1647 read: 'He dips women naked, in ye night, fit for works of darkness'; and the Calvinist clergyman, Daniel Featley, maintained that it was not unusual for Baptists to strip 'stark naked, not only when they flock in great multitudes, men and women together, to their Jordans to be dipped; but also upon other occasions, when the season permits'. The Puritan divine Richard Baxter accused John Tombes of wanting to baptize naked 'all the maids' of his Bewdley parish.

Partly on account of his name, Oates found himself a sitting target for the heresy-hunter Thomas Edwards, who recorded that, during a preaching tour of Essex in 1646, he 'hath been sowing his tares, booltmong, and wild Oates in these parts these five weeks without any control, hath seduced hundreds, and dipped many in Bocking River'. Oates, Edwards noted, 'traded chiefly with young women and young maids, dipping many of them'; other women 'were called out of their beds to go dipping in rivers', with Oates 'dipping many of them in the night, so that their husbands and masters could not keep them in their houses'. Edwards also accused Oates of using his evangelism to line his purse, conning the gullible into paying him for baptism. But Baptists could also respond in kind: when arraigned on one occasion for sexual misconduct during baptism, Lawrence Clarkson answered by appeal to experience which, he argued, taught 'that nature hath small desire of copulation in water'. When his accusers laughed he suggested that they rather weep 'for the unclean thoughts of your heart...'.

Dipping, particularly in winter, was widely believed to carry the risk of death and disease, and critics delighted to recount tales of illness and fatality following immersion. Edwards notes that Oates was once imprisoned on suspicion of contributing to the death of a young woman during baptism (in fact he was eventually acquitted), and baptism *en masse* came in for regular criticism on account of its potential to spread contagious diseases, such as the 'promiscuous Anabaptists' were known to have had. Immersion also provided opponents with plenty of scope for ridicule, written attacks on Baptists appearing under titles such as *The Anabaptist washed, washed and shrunk in the washing* and *The Dippers dipt. Or, the Anabaptists duck't and plunged Over Head and Eares* (this latter the work of the Reverend Featley, which went through three editions between 1642 and 1645). Unlike many real Anabaptists of the previous century, however, no English Baptist appears to have been called upon to suffer martyrdom by the obscenely symbolic method of drowning, although Edwards, with only thinly veiled delight, records one occasion at Dunmow when Oates was plucked from a house by 'some of the town' who 'threw him in the river, thoroughly dipping him'!

Dislike and fear of Baptists was grounded upon more than their practice of immersion, of course; like the Anabaptists before them, their insistence on the right to withdraw from established religion and set up their own separate independent churches, and on the duty of the state to recognize that right, was perceived to be deeply subversive of social cohesion. At the heart of their creed was a conviction that the New Testament laid down one model for the church – that of believers voluntarily gathering together – which it was the duty of all succeeding generations of believers to imitate. Thus the 'church' explicitly could not comprise all who lived in a 'parish', for these included both the saved and the reprobate (which was why paedo-baptism was so wrong). A church was a committed and converted group of men and women – 'a company of visible saints' as the 1644 *Confession* put it – consciously choosing to bond together and preserve their purity by applying their own membership criteria and code of discipline. A church was also to be maintained by the giving of its members, not a tax or tithe imposed on members and non-members alike. By rejecting the authority of established church, by being 'separated from the world by the Word and Spirit of God', as Helwys put it, and 'knit unto the Lord and unto one another by baptism', Baptists were easy targets in troubled times for those who saw them as a threat to society – or indeed, as an alternative society.

In addition, both the main Baptist doctrines relating to redemption – that all people had the same potentiality to be saved (Arminianism) or an 'elect' were chosen for salvation through no effort of their own (Calvinism) – pointed toward the essential equality of all people before God, and therefore to a rejection of hierarchical church structures in favour of more democratic ones. The 1644 Particular Baptist *Confession* made it clear that salvation did not depend on the merits of the individual, affirming that 'the tenders of the Gospel to the conversion of sinners is absolutely free, no way requiring as absolutely necessary any qualifications, preparations, terrors of the law or preceding ministry of the law but only and alone the naked soul as a sinner and ungodly to receive Christ'.

Further, a conviction that the individual is saved through the unmerited bestowal of divine favour – 'free grace' – might arouse suspicions that Baptists no longer considered themselves under the law: if a person had been chosen or 'elected' by God for salvation, then no sin that they could commit, however heinous, could undermine that transaction. Most Baptists, however, tended to deny that they were 'antinomian' – a term often linked by their accusers with 'Anabaptist' – in the sense of considering themselves above either the moral or civil law: obedience to the law, they argued, was the fruit of their belief. Yet some did stress the 'divinely enlightened conscience' above the moral law, and use this as a basis for rejecting those responsible for enforcing the latter, including bishops, clergy and synods.

Baptist churches generally knew of no distinction between clergy and laity: 'every disciple that hath ability is authorized, yea commanded, to preach, convert and baptize as well and as much (if not more) than a pastor', a document emanating from John Murton's church in 1620 put it. The Particular Baptist *Confession* of 1644 was explicit in saying that any 'preaching disciple' – not necessarily the pastor – could baptize, and laid down no rules pertaining to the administration of the Lord's Supper. In some Baptist churches the 'preaching disciple' could be female as well as male, a cause of scandal to many of their opponents. Mrs Attway is one who was known to have preached regularly in Baptist churches – first just to other women but subsequently at regularly weekday lectures which were said to have drawn a thousand listeners – and we might infer from Robert Baillie's description of her as 'the mistress of all the she-preachers in Coleman Street' and to 'other feminine preachers' in Kent and Norfolk, that the practice was widespread.

Henry Jessey recounted in a popular pamphlet, *The Exceeding Riches of Grace Advanced* (1647), the remarkable experience of Sarah Wight, a member of his congregation, who fasted for 75 days and was recognized by the church as an inspired and wise woman worthy to be consulted for spiritual advice. Wight, whose visions were not unlike those of the Fifth Monarchist Anna Trapnel, who visited her, reportedly described to fellow members of her congregation the deep experience she felt during her long fast in terms of Lazarus' 'four days in the grave', from which she had now 'risen to live with Jesus Christ'. 'Now I have my desire; I desired nothing but a crucified Christ and I have him ... I do eat, but it's meat to eat that the world knows not of ... His words were found, and I did eat them.' Elizabeth Poole, a member of Kiffin's church until her expulsion, was another visionary who once addressed an audience of parliamentary soldiers and appealed to Parliament to spare the king's life.

Baptist ministers were in most cases ordinary working people, elected by their fellow members. Known often as 'mechanick preachers' (though more than a few were former ordained clergy of the established church) they would, upon appointment, generally continue in their employment for six days of the week, thus ruling out the possibility that they might preach just to appease their 'paymasters' (which is how the 'beneficed clergy' were popularly perceived). The democratic nature of their appointment also meant that it was not they but the ordinary members who had the upper hand in the church. The right to preach conferred no authority upon any member chosen for the task, and in contrast to the practice of the established church, whose university-educated parsons generally expected to be listened to in a spirit of deference and awe, discussion of sermons seems to have been a regular occurrence in Baptist churches. Mrs Attway, whose trade was selling lace, was one who regularly invited objections to her sermons, and at Bell Alley church in London, where often there were several preachers 'on offer', the congregation would shout out which ones they preferred and then debate with them during and after their sermons.

Thomas Edwards noted that, not only was it 'usual and lawful ... for the company to stand up and object against the doctrine delivered when the exerciser of his gifts hath made an end, but in the midst of it, so that sometimes upon some standing up and objecting, there's pro and con for almost an hour, and falling out among themselves before the man can have finished his discourse'. Sometimes there was 'such a confusion and noise, as if it were a play; and some will be speaking here, some there'. In addition to ministers, the office of 'apostle' or 'messenger' – a 'travelling evangelist' called to make converts and plant or build up churches – was also known in some General Baptist circles. These also supported themselves by their trade.

It is not difficult to see how such democratic and egalitarian practices laid Baptists open to attack from both the church and the state. If the two institutions were linked, as White says, 'by one unquestioned partnership in which the church supplied the cement of a common faith and the divine validation of the accustomed forms of society',[5] then lack of adherence to the one was by implication rejection of the authority of the other. And it was not just individual priests in those parishes where Baptists and other sectaries formed their own churches who felt threatened, as their spiritual authority and the cohesion of their parish were undermined: the Baptists' philosophy of separation and independence, and encouragement to others similarly to disengage from the church, undermined the whole fabric of society and troubled and angered many at all levels of the community. 'None but rogues would put down Common Prayer' a Somerset constable affirmed, adding that he hoped to see Thomas Collier – who had established a Baptist congregation in Taunton in the 1640s – and his friends hanged because they 'would not go to church'.

The assumption underpinning the Elizabethan Settlement was that baptism acquired for the newly born both membership of the church and citizenship of the country: Baptists not only rejected infant baptism but insisted that every person had the right to choose which church (if any) they would join, even if (or perhaps especially) that involved rejection of the one into which they had been baptized at birth. And the consequences of this, as the sometime Baptist Samuel Fisher recognized, were far-reaching in the extreme: 'Once give over christening the whole parish infancy, and then farewell that parish posture which the Pope set up in all Christendom some six hundred years ago, yea then falls down the parochial-steeple-house, priesthood, pay and all.' 'Infant baptism upholds a national church', as Christopher Blackwood, founder of a number of Baptist churches in Ireland put it, 'as because if that were taken away, a national church would fall down'.

In the 1640s, as so many familiar social, political and ecclesiastical landmarks gradually disappeared, the Baptists' overt rejection of the church made them a deeply subversive force. As R. J. Acheson comments, if Baptists were perceived to be threatening the whole parish structure of the church, 'and at a time when the whole world seemed to be shifting on its axis ... it is no wonder that the non-Baptist majority, which longed for settlement and stability, should have reacted so strongly against a sect which threatened to disrupt traditional society for ever'.[6] Their refusal to pay the tithe, encouragement to others to do the same, and advocacy of an end to that whole system, threatened in an intensely practical way the continuance of the church's presence and power.

Furthermore, the practice each local church adopted of appointing their own minister, accountable only to them, limited the national church's potential to act as an agent of social control through the dissemination of the policies and ideas of the ruler or monarch of the day. Charles I was hardly the first monarch to understand that 'people are governed by the pulpit more than the sword in time of peace', and not only did Baptists practise and encourage a boycott of the church and its preaching, they appointed their own untrained – and therefore politically unreliable – preachers to expound to them the word, and actively developed a culture of debate and argument around each sermon! And some of these preachers, to the consternation of arch-conformists like Edwards, were women!

Baptists, then, suffered considerably at the hands of both the church and the state. Just as the first returnees from the continent met the full force of Archbishop Bancroft's campaign to enforce conformity, so many of their successors were caught up in the drive in the 1630s by Bancroft's successor but one, William Laud, to erase all traces of Puritanism. Some of the most severe attacks on Baptist congregations took place in the early 1640s, with numerous gatherings – usually in private houses – being broken up, sometimes violently. Spilsbury's church in east London was one of those attacked, he and around 30 others being arrested and found guilty of 'with malicious and seditious intent at Radcliffe in Stepney holding an unlawful assembly and conventicle for the exercise of religion in contempt of the laws'. This was in September 1641. A few months previously Thomas Lambe had been arrested with others at a meeting in Whitechapel by a justice and his mob who, Lambe claimed, armed with swords and clubs, 'violently entered the house encouraging thereby many scores of persons to beat down our windows with stones'.

In the same year a meeting at the house of one Peter Golding in London was invaded by a gang operating on the instructions of the Mayor who 'beat, thrust, pinched and kicked such men and women as fled not his handling'. A similar fate befell other Baptist congregations and leaders in London, including Edward Barber, who was sent to Newgate for his opposition to infant baptism and paying the tithe. And repression of Baptists was not limited to the capital: one Thomasine Scott was imprisoned in Beccles in Suffolk in 1644 for having 'refused to go to church, confessing she was an anabaptist'. The Particular Baptist leaders acknowledged in their 1644 *Confession* the danger that their beliefs placed them in, noting the desire of their opponents, 'if they can find the place of our meeting, to get together in clusters to stone us, as looking upon us as a people holding such things as that we are not worthy to live'.

But many Baptists were eager to discourage the belief that in pursuing religious liberty they were also fomenting political instability. Calvinistic Baptists were particularly keen to portray themselves as respectable and law-abiding, and stress that they harboured no subversive or disloyal intent, and the *Confession of Faith* issued by their churches in 1644 affirmed that 'King and Parliament freely chosen by the kingdom' were to be 'acknowledged, reverenced and obeyed, according to godliness; not because of wrath only but for conscience sake'. The framers of this document, who included Kiffin and Spilsbury, were clearly unhappy to be depicted as 'disclaiming of magistracy' and as people 'lying under that calumny and black band of heretics, and sowers of division': they wanted to stress the orthodoxy of their position and true status as law-abiding bodies of the Lord's people, not a subversive network of insurrectionists. They may also have been anxious to keep in with the increasingly influential Independent churches, seeing in that alliance their best hope of securing their aims. Three years after the publication of the *Confession*, Jessey, Kiffin and Knollys were signatories to another document which affirmed the duty of the civil magistrate to act as God's agent for good order, together with the principles of private property and the division of men and women into 'several subordinate ranks and degrees'. Particular Baptists were also to be found in 1647 attempting to bring about a negotiated settlement between Charles and the Army – an arrangement which, as one contemporary source noted, 'was admirably suited to remove from Baptists the taint of being rebels'.

Particular Baptists' leaders also separated from the Levellers once they perceived the latter's stance to have become more radical. Their churches had originally given their active support to the Leveller cause: Levellers were, after all, major champions of the cause of religious toleration; but in 1647 eight leading pastors and laymen joined forces with the Congregational societies to produce a document highly critical of the movement. Then, in March 1649, Kiffin, Spilsbury and several other pastors added salt to the wound by producing a petition which specifically disavowed the Levellers' newly issued pamphlet, *The Second Part of Englands New Chaines discovered*. This contained a scathing attack on the army grandees in the wake of 'Pride's Purge', the forcible debarring from Parliament of those MPs committed to continuing discussions with the king, and the Particular Baptists were at pains to stress that their churches' meetings 'are not at all to intermeddle with the ordering or altering civil government (which we humbly and sub-missively leave to the supreme power) but solely for the advance-ment of the gospel'. To underline the point, the document also emphasized their differences with the German Anabaptists of the previous century.

The Leveller leaders saw this as little short of a betrayal, but the mood darkened even further in April when one of the petition's authors, William Kiffin, produced the bitterly *ad hominem* tract *Walwyn's Wiles*. Kiffin may have been enraged by Walwyn's pam-phlet *Vanitie of the Present Churches*, published two months earlier and containing a forceful attack on some of the beliefs and prac-tices of separatist churches, but the Particular Baptists' dislike for the Levellers was now abundantly clear – and reinforced still fur-ther when another critical tract co-authored with the Congregationalists appeared in 1651. Stephen Wright has argued that, between 1647 and 1649, Kiffin and other Particular Baptist leaders in London 'stood clearly and positively against the political

20

radicals and on the side of socially conservative forces', deliberately co-ordinating their action for maximum political effect. Certainly to the Levellers it looked like their one-time friends were now 'conniving with government politicians interested in discrediting them'.[7]

Yet among the General Baptists, including the leadership, there was much overt support for the Levellers. In fact, so much did the Levellers owe to Baptist churches in terms of personnel and organization that more than one scholar has suggested that the Levellers 'might be regarded as the political wing of the Baptist movement'![8] That General Baptists were drawn more from the 'middling sort' of people may be one explanation for their attraction to a more radical solution to the political crisis of the 1640s, and they were certainly less in touch with the mainstream Independents than their Calvinistic cousins. One congregation particularly noted for its Leveller sympathies was Thomas Lambe's, which played an important role in compiling and distributing the first Leveller document, *A Remonstrance of Many Thousand Citizens*, with its call for an end to tithes and limitations on the powers of the king and House of Lords. The Leveller leader William Walwyn noted that this document had been framed 'by the generality of congregations'. Another General Baptist leader associated with this document, and in fact imprisoned for his role in supporting it, was Jeremiah Ives, while Samuel Oates worked to promote the Levellers' 'Agreement of the People' in Rutland (where, incidentally, his better known son, Titus, was born in 1649).

Another leading Baptist and Leveller was Henry Denne. A close associate of Lambe and regular at the Bell Alley meeting, Denne was one of the four Levellers convicted after the failed Army mutiny in 1649 and sentenced to be shot at Burford. Unlike his three colleagues, Denne publicly recanted and was pardoned and spared, and he later went into print to explain his actions, regretting that he had failed 'to yield obedience unto that authority under which we are placed'. Denne was instrumental in founding Baptist churches in Fenstanton and Warboys. Edward Barber was another General Baptist who openly supported the Levellers, his London congregation being described in 1643 as 'factious movers of sedition and rebellion, and the cause of these unnatural wars, and of differences betwixt his majesty and parliament'. Edmund Chillenden and Robert Everard – the latter referred to as 'Buff Coat' in the record of the Putney debates – were also both General Baptists and Levellers with a military background.

Of the Leveller leadership, Richard Overton appears to have had the closest links with Baptists. The author of a book arguing against the survival of the human soul beyond death, *Mans Mortalitie* (1643), Overton played a key role in a debate on the subject in February 1646 involving the Baptist leaders Thomas Lambe and Timothy Batte. Overton also had a connection with Lambe's congregation through one of its leading members, Thomas Tew (or Tue), who once confessed in the Fleet prison to having a printing press in his house which Overton used (and on which two of Lilburne's tracts were printed). Overton's opponents also noted his Baptist links, Edwards describing him in *Gangraena* as an Anabaptist, a term used also of him by the House of Lords in 1646. Overton may have left the Baptists before the Levellers emerged, but he, Lilburne and other leading Levellers maintained steady contact with Baptists in the 1640s. On many points the concerns of the two movements overlapped – removal of tithes, freedom of religion, reform of the law and courts – even if some Baptists, particularly those who harboured millenarian hopes, found that the Levellers' advocacy of a secular state opened up a gap between them ultimately too wide to bridge.

While Baptists joined with many of their contemporaries in welcoming Cromwell's government, rejoicing when it abolished compulsory attendance at parish worship, they also shared the widespread disillusionment when it failed to deliver the full raft of hoped-for reforms, including, notably, the abolition of tithes. The year 1653, when the high hopes invested in the Barebones Parliament were dashed and Cromwell was made Lord Protector, tested the patience of many, particularly those who thought all trappings of monarchy had disappeared with Charles Stuart. Some leading Baptists, like Henry Jessey, joined the emerging Fifth

Monarchy Movement, which embodied hopes for further radical reform and was critical of Oliver for usurping Jesus in making himself sole ruler; others, however, such as Kiffin, Spilsbury and Joseph Sansom took the line that the Protector's actions were necessary and that strong leadership was vital. Kiffin and other Particular Baptists issued a letter in January 1654 accusing the Fifth Monarchists of bringing 'shame and contempt to the whole nation' and recalling the tyranny of others who had claimed a divine right to rule, such as the late king. Kiffin played a key role in dissuading Baptist churches from following the Fifth Monarchist line, and many Particular Baptists feared that any sign of support for the movement would encourage the belief that they denied authority and 'would pull down all magistracy'. In 1657 Spilsbury, Sansom, Knollys and Jessey – though not Kiffin, by then a Member of Parliament – were moved to write in passionate terms dissuading Cromwell from accepting the crown, on the grounds that restoring the institution of monarchy would be 'destructive to the safety and liberty of the people'. They feared that such a move would imply a belief that, because God had not yet perfected his work, 'therefore we must return to Egypt'.

At the end of 1659, with Cromwell dead and the restoration of the monarchy more than a distant possibility, Baptists came together in a rare display of political unity to affirm their willingness to 'live peaceably' under whatever government shall be established. The following year they underlined their quietist stance still further by issuing statements distancing themselves from the Fifth Monarchists and disavowing their earlier enthusiasm for regime change. For some of their opponents, like the Quaker Richard Hubberthorne, this was a huge sign of weakness: 'If Charles Stuart come, or any other and establish popery and govern by tyranny, you have begged pardon by promising willingly to submit and live peaceably under it as the ordinance of God ... Some did judge that ye had been of another spirit,' he wrote.

Yet the Baptists' statements reiterated no less strongly their earlier opposition to any attempt by the king to prohibit freedom of worship, a stance guaranteed to deny them a quiet life in the ensuing years. And indeed, as the House of Stuart once again stamped its authority on the country, so Baptists found themselves once more subject to popular suspicion and distrust and arrested and tried – often as much on a whim and a rumour than on the basis of hard evidence of plots and dissension. In some cases Baptists were tried and executed on account of their part in the overthrow of Charles I or links with militant Fifth Monarchists, but others were clearly guilty of nothing more than thwarting the authorities' obsession with ecclesiastical unity and the need to ensure that the threat of another Münster, real or imagined, never materialized.

Baptists were strong on organization and discipline, and full of passion and commitment, yet their influence on the course of events in the 1640s and 1650s was at best indirect. With around 300 churches by 1660 and a membership of perhaps 25,000, they probably never represented more than 1 per cent of the population even at their height; but, more importantly, they also lacked any broad vision for society beyond their fundamental call for religious toleration. Baptist historian B. R. White goes so far as to suggest that, 'while the majority of the leading Calvinistic Baptists were probably republican in their political sentiments there must have been many who hardly had any political opinions at all'.[9] Certainly there were only a few like the Bristol Baptist Robert Purnell who thanked the Lord for taking 'princes and lords which were so high' and bringing 'their heads so low as to the block'.

Yet while many Baptists may have wished to avoid engagement with politics, in the 1640s they could not escape it altogether. What all Baptists sought, in addition to an end to tithing, was the liberty to worship according to their lights, and while they differed regarding the tactics necessary to achieve this, their deep conviction that this freedom was both right in itself and necessary for their survival drove them to seek alliances with the forces most likely to deliver it. They may not have tried to promote a platform with wide general appeal but, as White has argued, they 'could not help being deeply and personally involved politically. They had a vested interest in the kind of government which would guarantee a large measure of religious freedom such as Cromwell's religious policies provided.'[10]

We should not underestimate the extent to which Baptists were seen as subversive and a threat to good order, even if this can best be understood as the outworking of their democratic theology in a milieu which knew no distinction between 'religious' and 'political' questions, rather than the consequence of any overt political intent. It is, of course, to their credit that they survived when so many other sects and movements fell away, and this may be due not just to their ability to organize and maintain good order, but to the political acumen of a leadership able skilfully to negotiate, as Mark Bell has suggested, a middle course 'between the radical democracy of the Levellers and the radical theocracy of the Fifth Monarchists'.[11] If they lost members in time to those movements which might have been thought to be maintaining the radical potential they themselves once had – Quakers, Fifth Monarchists, possibly even the newly emerging Seventh-Day Baptists – they were clearly also able to attract and retain new converts. Perhaps their significance might also be measured in terms of the role they played in enabling many important figures, including leading Levellers, to cut their teeth before finding alternative outlets for their enthusiasm.

CHAPTER TWO

Levellers

WRITING FROM NEWGATE Prison, where he was being detained on the orders of the House of Lords, Richard Overton sought to remind his captors of some basic truths:

> *For by natural birth, all men are equally and alike born to like propriety, liberty and freedom, and as we are delivered of God by the hand of nature into this world, every one with a natural, innate freedom and propriety (as it were writ in the table of every man's heart, never to be obliterated) even so are we to live, every one equally and alike to enjoy his birthright and privilege; even all whereof God by nature hath made him free.*

The date is October 1646, and Overton develops in this treatise, *An Arrow Against All Tyrants And Tyrany*, an argument for political rights based largely on natural law. 'To every individual in nature, is given an individual property by nature, not to be invaded or usurped by any': for one person to deprive another of their individuality is a 'manifest violation and affront to the very principles of nature'.

The same month, from his cell a mile or two away in the Tower of London, John Lilburne writes a postscript to his tract *Londons Liberty in Chains*:

> *The omnipotent, glorious, and wise God, creating man for his own praise; made him more glorious [than] all the*

*rest of his creatures that he placed upon earth: creating
him in his own image ... and made him lord over the
earth, and all the things therein contained ... But made
him not lord, or gave him dominion over the individuals
of mankind, no further [than] by free consent, or
agreement, by giving up their power, each to other, for
their better being; so that originally, he gave no lordship,
nor sovereignty, to any of Adam's posterity, by will, and
prerogative, to rule over his brethren-men ...*

Drawing on both testaments of the Bible – this passage alone references six chapters in Genesis together with two of Paul's epistles –
Lilburne also explains his understanding of political rights. At
Creation, God endowed all humankind with equal status, empowering none to have dominion over another; and if history has been
littered with tyrannical and beastly acts, this is due to the Fall,
which Christ came to restore and repair. 'Christianity, or the
knowledge of Christ, doth not destroy morality, civility, justice, and
right reason; but rather restores it to its first perfection, beauty,
splendour and glory.'

These two writings alone should alert us to the danger of talking
about 'what Levellers believed' or 'the Leveller position'.
Considering the degree to which they organized themselves,
attracted mass support, produced political platforms, informed
high-level debate – and even raised funds through members' sub-
scriptions – it is tempting to see them as a prototype of a modern
political party. Yet, as Christopher Hill has said, 'the Levellers were
never a united, disciplined party or movement, as historians find to
their cost when they try to define their doctrines with any preci-
sion'.[1] There were core themes to their writings and campaigns, in
particular the rights and liberties of the individual; but their leaders
did not necessarily start from the same premises, nor always agree
about how the theoretical positions they shared should be applied.
Throughout their brief six-year existence their ideas were constantly
developing and evolving, and not only did they lack any 'chain of
command' to ensure that every member sang from the same hymnsheet, they had no fixed membership and no one hymnsheet!

28

In a sense it is hard to imagine how things might have been different. There was no 'party system' as we understand it today in the seventeenth century, and, as Frances Dow points out, 'the Levellers were not like a revolutionary party which had had a long period in opposition or in exile during which to assimilate and integrate various strands in its political thinking.'[2] Nor did they see themselves as the equivalent of a prospective party of government – in fact, quite the opposite, for since their platform represented 'an unanimous and universal resolution of all well-minded people' there would be, once it was adopted, no necessity for political activity based on party interest. Both leaders and followers were thrown together in the middle of a crisis which was itself in constant flux, and political coherence had, of necessity, to take second place to the need for an urgent response to the prevailing situation. In the rapidly changing context, tracts and speeches needed to be produced quickly to seize the moment and reach a particular audience, whether the army, the citizenry or Parliament. And the leaders themselves – chiefly Lilburne, Overton and William Walwyn, but also Thomas Prince, Samuel Chidley, William Larner, Mary Overton, Elizabeth Lilburne, John Wildman and others – varied widely in skills, temperament and discernment.

The Levellers first came to prominence in July 1646 with the publication of *A Remonstrance of Many Thousand Citizens*, setting out their main demands in terms of religious toleration and reform of Parliament. On its cover was an engraving of Lilburne set behind bars, an allusion to the imprisonment which prevented him from signing the document. Lilburne would have been well known at that time, having achieved a degree of notoriety even before linking up with Overton and Walwyn around 1645. In 1638, when only in his early twenties, he had been caught distributing seditious pamphlets and sentenced by the Star Chamber to be flogged, pilloried and imprisoned. These pamphlets had been specifically targeted at the bishops, and Lilburne maintained a loathing of the Anglican Church and its priests, and a belief in the separation of church and state, throughout his life.

Released from prison in 1641, Lilburne continued to campaign publicly against the church and the House of Lords, before joining the Parliamentary army and seeing active service against Prince Rupert in London and at the battle of Marston Moor. Though helped by Cromwell at significant stages in his early career, Lilburne had run-ins with other leaders of the army, and his imprisonment in the Tower in 1646–47, on the orders of the House of Lords, was linked to his quarrels with the Earl of Manchester and Colonel Edward King. (He spent so much of his life on the inside of that building that he and his wife Elizabeth even named one of their children, born during one of his absences, Tower.) Driven by religious convictions more than most Levellers, Lilburne held to an orthodox Calvinist theology until his conversion to Quakerism in later life, peppering his tracts with biblical references and allusions in support of his arguments. In the tract in which he records his conversion to Quakerism, *The Resurrection of John Lilburne* (1656), he gives the Scriptural warrant for his experience of discovering the light within.

Overton seems to have spent a good deal of the early 1640s engaged in clandestine printing and publishing, an industry which his wife Mary continued during his imprisonment. While his writing appears more rational and secular in tone than Lilburne's, Overton was a General Baptist for at least a part of his life and, in 1644, published a controversial book entitled *Mans Mortalitie*, arguing (as did many Anabaptists and John Milton) that the human soul perishes with the body at death and is only restored, with the body, at the general resurrection. Some of his most incisive and witty writings were attacks on the Presbyterian divines written under the pseudonym Martin Marpriest. Modelled on the work of the Elizabethan satirist 'Martin Marprelate', these tracts exposed the hypocrisy and high-living of churchmen – with their 'godly care for their own guts' and love of 'delicate, toothsome tithes' – while powerfully making the case for religious toleration: it is from his home in Toleration Street that Martin takes his pop at Sir John Presbyter and Sir Simon Synod. Even when writing his last tract, *The Baiting of the Great Bull of Bashan*, from the confines of the Tower, Overton's wit did not desert him, this writing containing some graphic references to Levellers snapping at the pox-ridden genitals of their opponents.

Walwyn's route into the Levellers also came through his concern with religious toleration, an issue on which he was actively campaigning in the early 1640s and on which he had written a tract, *The Humble Petition of the Brownists*. A possibly less colourful character than Lilburne or Overton, and more measured and intellectual in his writing, Walwyn produced some original and powerful pamphlets, including five rebutting the author of *Gangraena*, Thomas Edwards, who referred to him as 'a dangerous man, a stronghead'. Walwyn's intellectualism led him into debates about the faith and (as with Overton) frequent accusations of atheism, a charge he denied in *A still and soft voice from the Scriptures, witnessing them to be the word of God*. Walwyn admitted experiencing crises in his religious life, and he tended to eschew denominational labels, but he did acknowledge having embraced a form of 'antinomianism' in his early life, by which he meant 'that art of doctrine … of free justification by Christ alone'.

Walwyn was clear that Scripture contained much of value, insights that the Apostles have left us regarding the mind and will of God. 'I carry with me in all places a touch-stone that tryeth all things, and labours to hold nothing but what upon plain grounds appeareth good and useful', he wrote in *A Whisper in the eare of Mr Thomas Edwards* (1646): 'there are plain useful doctrines sufficient to give peace to my mind: direction and comfort to my life'. Walwyn's ability to make things happen 'behind the scenes', together with his inscrutability and cleverness, made him the most disliked of the Leveller leaders among the movement's opponents. One anonymous pamphleteer compared him to Thomas Müntzer, 'that Arch-Anabaptist', and in 1649 he was the subject of a nasty *ad hominem* attack by seven Puritan divines, including the Particular Baptist William Kiffin, entitled *Walwyn's Wiles*.

If we can talk about a Leveller philosophy, at its heart was the idea that all people were created equal and that no one had any God-given or natural right to govern or rule over another. As Lilburne wrote in *The Free Man's Freedom Vindicated*,

> *Every particular and individual man and woman that ever breathed in the world since [Adam and Eve] are and were by nature all equal and alike in power, dignity, authority and majesty, none of them having (by nature) any authority dominion or magisterial power, one over ... another.*

Rule of one person over another could only be tolerated where the governed had given their consent: governments could act only by the will of the people, and in *the people* resided ultimate sovereignty. 'A Parliamentary authority is a power intrusted by the people (that chose them) for their good, safety, and freedom', wrote Walwyn in *Englands Lamentable Slaverie* (October 1645), 'and therefore a Parliament cannot justly do any thing, to make the people less safe or less free, than they found them...'.

To many Levellers and others, of course, the government to which the nation was subject in the 1640s precisely did *not* reflect the will of the majority of the people. The question therefore raised was how could government be reconstituted so that the 'sovereignty of the people' could be expressed, and who, for that matter, were 'the people' in a political sense? It was in response to these questions that the Levellers produced their manifestoes, giving each the title 'An Agreement of the People' to indicate that, far from being mere rhetoric, their aim was to establish popular consent to a new form of government.

For Levellers, in order for Parliament to be more truly representative of the people's interests, two basic things had to happen: its undemocratic elements had to be stripped of their power, and those which were formally democratic had to be made more so in practice. As many people acknowledged, the undemocratic elements were the king and the House of Lords, and in their *Remonstrance of Many Thousand Citizens*, addressed to the Commons in 1646, the Leveller leaders made plain to their readers what they looked to it to do. 'We do expect', they wrote, 'that ye should ... show the intolerable inconveniences of having a kingly government ... and ... publish your resolution ... to acquit us of so great a charge and trouble forever.' In the case of the Lords, a body not chosen by the people but 'intruders, thrust upon us by kings', the Commons should likewise 'free us from their negative voice, or else tell us that it is reasonable we should be slaves'. The title of Overton's 1646 tract *An alarum to the house of lords against their insolent usurpation of the Common Liberties* really said it all.

A concomitant concern of the Levellers was to make the one institution which *did* purport to represent the people *more* representative. One failing of the present system, as Lilburne pointed out in 1646, was that it made no effort to ensure that every region of the country was equally represented: everybody had to pay taxes, but not everybody was represented in Parliament. 'It is unrighteous', Lilburne wrote during the Long Parliament, 'that Cornwall should choose fifty members and Yorkshire twice as big and three times as populous and rich not half so many and my own poor county, the bishopric of Durham, none at all.' The remedy was a redistribution of seats, with each county choosing 'a proportionable number suitable to the rates that county by their book of rates are assessed to pay towards the defraying of the public charge of the kingdom'. Greater accountability could also be ensured by more frequent elections (the first 'Agreement of the People' (1647) called for Parliament to be elected biennially, the third 'Agreement' (1649) annually); measures to reduce the corrupt practice of candidates 'buying' votes to get elected; the introduction of modest salaries for MPs to prevent their having to be dependent on rich patrons; and an extension of the franchise to embrace all men aged 21 and above, excepting servants, recipients of alms, and supporters of the king (who were required to wait ten years).

The Levellers' response to the question, 'who is to get the vote' – who, in other words, are 'the people' – provides an example of how their positions developed over time. The extension of the franchise to include 'all men of the age of one and twenty years and upwards (not being servants, or receiving alms, or having served the late king in arms or voluntary contributions)' was the position they had reached by the time of the third 'Agreement', published on

1 May 1649; but eighteen months before, in *The Case of the Armie Truly Stated*, they had petitioned simply that 'all the freeborn at the age of twenty one years and upwards, be the electors'. At Putney, during the debates with the army grandees, Thomas Rainsborough appeared to echo this view when he famously argued that 'the poorest he that is in England hath a life to live as the greatest he, and therefore ... I think it's clear, that every man that is to live under a government ought first by his own consent to put himself under that government', though another Leveller, Maximilian Petty, exposed a possible rift within the movement by suggesting only that 'all inhabitants that have not lost their birthright should have an equal voice in elections'. This might have excluded not just criminals and former royalists ('delinquents') but servants and recipients of alms, and such an exclusion, with the addition of those 'receiving wages from any particular person', appears in the second Leveller 'Agreement', dated December 1648 (which also limits the franchise to 'housekeepers'; that is, heads of households). If, as is generally accepted, the drafters of the Leveller manifestoes understood by 'servants' people 'in service' and apprentices, and not wage-earners living in their own homes, the third 'Agreement' represents a return to a more inclusive stance.

Commentators have debated for years what Levellers might have meant by terms like 'servant' and 'birthright', and it is possible to make the differences among them appear greater than perhaps they were: Petty was a somewhat peripheral figure in Leveller circles, and other Leveller spokespeople at Putney were fairly consistent in calling for something like universal male suffrage. In a sense the second 'Agreement' was not really a Leveller document but a compromise worked out with other parties, including Ireton and other army officers, in the hope of attracting army support. There is also the point, raised more recently by Edward Vallance, that Rainsborough possibly did not have voting in mind at all when making his famous speech at Putney, but was referring to the moment when the Levellers' 'Agreement', 'like an oath of loyalty to the new regime, would be tendered to the nation for subscription, when all men would choose whether to put themselves "under the government"'.[3]

It is also of interest that not once does the movement appear to have considered whether women should be entitled to vote, despite the high profile of Katherine Chidley, Elizabeth Lilburne and other women within the movement, and even the publication of *A Petition of Women* affirming their 'equal interest with the men of this nation in those liberties and securities' identified in other of the movement's pamphlets. Extending the franchise to women was surely a corollary of their belief in the fundamental equality of all people under God, and entirely consistent with their stance that no one should put themselves under a government to which they have not themselves been able to give consent. Even their arch-critic Thomas Edwards pointed out that this principle granted women exemption from the 'jurisdiction of the House of Commons', and, indeed, 'all youths who were under age at the beginning of this Parliament'. What *is* consistent about the Levellers' position, however, is its focus on the importance of votes being independently cast: voters must be free from influence by others, including employers, landlords and (here we see them as people of their time) heads of households. They wanted a fairer society for all 'free-born Englishmen', but may have concluded that, among those who had lost their liberty, in this case upon marriage, were women. Yet even here, even if they could not conceive of wives ever being heads of the house, they might have considered the position of widows (though this is, of course, to impose modern-day assumptions upon them).

Leveller experience of the way that those with power, and those aspiring to gain power, used that power, led them to press for clear limitations on governmental authority. Government was necessary, as Walwyn affirmed in *A Manifestation* (1649), because 'we know very well the pravity and corruption of man's heart is such that there could be no living without it'; but this pravity and corruption was as evident among those in power as in those they ruled – indeed, as Wildman once said, the magistrate is 'more probable to err than the people that have no power in their hands'. Levellers had no doubt that 'power corrupts', and that the people should only cede so much to their rulers: and because they knew 'by wofull experience' the tendency of power to make rulers 'pervert the same to their own domination, and to the prejudice our peace and liberties', Levellers argued that there were certain fundamental rights which even the most truly representative Parliament should not be free to touch. These included the right to practise religion as one wished, the right not to be conscripted into the navy or army against one's conscience, and the right to be treated equally under the law.

Freedom of conscience had been a concern of Leveller leaders before the movement came into being, and it infused their collective writings. It was vital in the area of belief and worship: 'matters of religion and the ways of God's worship, are not at all entrusted to any human power' they affirmed in the first 'Agreement', 'because therein we cannot remit or exceed a tittle of what our consciences dictate to be the mind of God, without wilful sin'. 'The inward man is God's prerogative; the outward man is man's prerogative', wrote Overton in 1647, a view shared by Walwyn, who made a distinction between 'things natural', which were under civil government's jurisdiction, and 'things supernatural', which were under God's. Levellers were clear that everyone had the right to make up their own mind in matters of religion and not be compelled by another.

The issue was complex, though, and Levellers had to agree that 'freedom to practise religion' could not encompass behaviour that was 'destructive to humane society' or could endanger the state: a person claiming their religion entitled them to commit a criminal act such as murder, or to offend against 'public modesty, comeliness, and civility', would have to have their freedom curtailed. On such occasions, natural law would trump 'religious law'. But Levellers did hold that religious toleration must extend to all, including Jews, Muslims and those accused of atheism and idolatry – a radically consistent position at a time when many of their contemporaries still considered celebration of the Catholic Mass to be a criminal offence and there was a concern in high places to clamp down on extreme forms of religion. Overton also made a highly unconventional plea for 'Papist and Protestant' to 'love one another' and live in peace.

Many other groups pursued religious liberty, of course, and for some it was fundamental to their very existence; but not all saw that it was the other side of the coin from political liberty. Levellers *did* make that connection, and in this sense they stand out from many of their contemporaries. As Brian Manning has said, 'it may be argued whether the Levellers' ultimate aim was religious liberty, for which political liberty was the means, or whether their overriding objective was political liberty, for which religious liberty was the means', but they certainly understood that the two could not be separated.[4]

Levellers shared the disdain which all radicals felt for the clergy of the established church. Like many of their contemporaries they believed that religion was used by those in power to keep the people in order, with the clergy playing a vital part by preaching up the doctrines of obedience and submission to governments. In one of his pre-Leveller writings, *The Compassionate Samaritane* (1644), Walwyn argued that the clergy deliberately distorted the simple message of the gospel for their own gain: their insistence that only university-educated men were entitled to preach enabled them to monopolize interpretation of the Scriptures and, 'by politic glosses and comments', introduce another gospel 'suitable to [their] covetous, ambitious and persecuting spirit'. The clergy had no real concern for the interests of the common people, merely the maintenance of their own rights, privileges and income. With many others, Levellers believed that, as Walwyn put it in one of his responses to Thomas Edwards, God did not choose the learned to be his prophets and preachers but 'herdsmen, fishermen, tent-makers, toll-gatherers, etc'; and just as such people were perfectly able to understand and participate in politics if given the opportunity, so they could comprehend the Bible themselves if they 'would but take boldness to themselves and not distrust their own understandings'.

Levellers seem consistently to have held that no one ought to be compelled to attend a state church, pay tithes to it, or in any way conform to it – although they did submit, in their first 'Agreement of the People' (1647), that there may be a case for governments 'instructing' the public in matters of religion, provided it were not done with compulsion. They shared the concern felt by many dissenting groups when, in the wake of the overthrow of the bishops, Parliament set about establishing another national church, with all that that would mean in terms of lack of freedom and toleration for sects and 'gathered' churches (from whom they drew much of their support). Thus in the third 'Agreement' of 1649 Levellers called explicitly for parishioners to have the right to choose for themselves their ministers and agree the terms of their appointment, rather than have those ministers paid through a compulsory tithe – measures which amounted to a *de facto* separation of church and state.

Equal treatment for all under the law was another issue that Levellers pressed, and in their third 'Agreement' they called for an end to all 'privileges or exemptions of any persons from the laws'. Leveller tracts constantly attacked the privileges enjoyed by members of the Lords and Commons, who have the right to send others to prison and subject them to torture 'without showing cause', but are themselves above the law in that they cannot be sued for debt and are free from the general obligation to pay taxes. What is more, Levellers pointed out, the ordinary people who *are* subject to all the laws are generally prevented from knowing their rights by virtue of those laws still being couched in Latin and Norman French – or in some cases not even written at all, but based supposedly on 'precedent'. The summons which a person might receive, and the nature of the charge laid against them, would often be in a foreign tongue, and this, together with the exorbitant fees which lawyers were wont to charge, often resulted in many ordinary people being left with no defence. Levellers made it one of their persistent demands that the law, 'locked up from common capacities in the Latin or French tongues' be translated into the vernacular so that 'the meanest English commoner', who could read his or her own language, might be able to understand the laws under which they were governed. Just as ordinary people were now allowed to read the Bible for themselves and discover its meaning, so they should be empowered to comprehend the law.

That some English laws had been framed in French was, of course, a consequence of the Norman invasion, and Levellers shared with contemporaries such as Winstanley the view that 1066 was not only a significant rupture in English history, but had brought about an end both to the liberties enjoyed in Anglo-Saxon times and the representative institutions which enshrined those liberties. According to the popular 'myth of the Norman yoke', the bondage from which the English people now strove to free themselves – the whole nexus of king, nobles, gentry, lawyers, landowners, clergy and the like – came in under William, and the opportunity must be taken now to dismantle it. While they valued the freedoms achieved under Magna Carta, Levellers believed that the law was part of the Norman bondage and should be thoroughly reformed to give the people back the liberties which they had lost at the Conquest.

Leveller tracts called for freedom from arbitrary arrest and imprisonment without trial, and the right to trial by an independent jury, free of any party interest. One of England's 'new chains' discovered by Lilburne, in his 1649 pamphlet of that name, was the high court of justice 'whereby that great and strong hold of our preservation, the way of trial by twelve sworn men of the neighbourhood, is infringed, all liberty of exception against the tryers is over-ruled by a court consisting of persons picked and chosen in an unusual way'. As Frances Dow perceptively points out, arguments focused on the recovery of rights which used to exist were not entirely consistent with those based on the pursuit of rights because they ought to exist – natural rights – and this accounts for 'the transitional nature of much Leveller thinking, and their Janus-like use of extant political theories to point in new radical and even progressive directions'.[5]

Levellers also held freedom of the press to be fundamental, in order to guarantee both political and religious liberty. A free press was essential if governments were to be held to account and their 'trecherous and tyranical designs' exposed and prevented, Lilburne maintained. Levellers therefore called for an end to the licensing of the press, on the grounds that suppression of the truth led to the people being kept in ignorance and the nation enslaved to tyrants and oppressors: 'for what may not be done to that people who may not speak or write, but at the pleasure of licensers?' asked the Levellers following the appointment of new judges to license pamphlets in January 1649.

It is sometimes overlooked that Levellers called for democratic reforms at local as well as national level. Among their demands were that local communities be allowed to elect their own officials and officers, who would be much more responsive to the popular will and more easily held to account; that justice be administered through local law courts by locally elected judicial officials; that local militias be established to replace the centralized professional army; and that ministers in parish churches be elected by the parishioners themselves. Such policies were consistent with their belief in the sovereignty of the people and concern to prevent power being concentrated in a small number of people in central government: they saw that what we would now call 'decentralization' would better ensure the protection of individual rights and freedoms, and they may even have envisaged that power administered locally would ultimately have more significance in people's lives than that wielded by any central government.

The Levellers' commitment to defending the rights and liberties of 'the people' is clear in all their writings and speeches, yet predominantly it was the 'middling' sort of people whose interests exercised them – 'the hobnails, clouted shoes, the private soldiers, the leather and woollen aprons, and the labourers and industrious people of England' as Lilburne described them in 1653. It was, after all, largely from these ranks that their leaders themselves came. Yet some of the Leveller leaders do also demonstrate a deep concern for the plight of the 'miserable, distressed, starved' thousands, and some of their statements angrily expose the gross inequalities in income between the rich and the poor. 'Poor men, that have not bread to still the cry of their children, must either pay or go in person to the wars', wrote Overton in *The Arraignement of Mr Persecution* (1645), 'while those devouring Church-lubbers live at ease, feed on dainties, neither pay nor go themselves, but preach out our very hearts.' In answer to the charge of his critics that he was unhappy 'that some abound whilst others want bread', Walwyn affirmed that he did indeed 'think it a sad thing, in so fruitful a land, as through God's blessing, this is' and that it was 'one main end of government, to provide, that those who refuse not labour, should eat comfortably'. Lilburne denounced the 'pomp, superfluities, and debauchery' of the rich, and Walwyn the silks, beavers and rings of those Christians who have 'more than sufficeth': 'the wants and distresses of the poor will testify that the love of God they have not', he wrote.

Yet if the Leveller leaders thought that the rich were to blame for the situation of the poor, they had no appetite for economic measures to redistribute wealth or land; rather, they upheld the right of the individual to own property, with all the social and economic inequalities that that might entail, and spelled out explicitly in documents like *The Humble Petition* of September 1648, and third 'Agreement' the following year, that no representative of the people should have any power 'to level men's estates, destroy propriety, or make all things common'. Lilburne, in fact, profoundly despised what he called 'this conceit of levelling of property and magistracy', calling it 'so ridiculous and foolish an opinion ... because it would, if practised, destroy not only all industry in the world, but raze the very foundation of government'. Their nomenclature had been thrust upon them against their will – they were, as they often said, 'commonly (though unjustly) called Levellers' – and they were especially keen to rebuff any suggestion that their label was to be understood in any literal, economic sense, or that they had any similarities to the Diggers or 'True Levellers'. (An exception was the authors of the Leveller tracts *Light Shining in Buckinghamshire* and *More Light Shining in Buckinghamshire*, whose views did appear to be much closer to those of the Diggers). Yet they were not complacent about the need for practical measures to ensure that no one would have to beg, and saw potential for economic change when the rich were converted to 'practical

Christianity', to a realization that the essence of the gospel comprised good works.

But just as they believed that the roots of the people's oppression were political, so they saw political rather than economic reform as the way forward; at the end of the day it was less 'the poor' who stood to gain from the sort of political changes they advocated than the small trades-people. Rather than pursue economic equality they sought to expand the opportunities for economic advancement for the small tenant farmer, the craftsperson, the trader: unlike the Diggers, they had no vision of common ownership to offer the landless labourer, the squatter, the cottager. We 'never had it in our thoughts to level men's estates', they wrote in the wake of the Diggers' occupation of St George's Hill in April 1649, 'it being the utmost of our aim that ... every man with as much security as may be enjoy his property.'

How central were theological beliefs in shaping the views of the Leveller leaders? The rational, 'natural law' and historical basis of their ideas might give the impression that religious thinking was not influential, and David Loades has a point when he asserts that 'almost uniquely among Civil War radical groups, they did not place religion at the centre of their arguments.'[6] Yet Thomas Edwards, who devoted part of the third volume of his *Gangraena* to an attack on Leveller principles, was clear that the emergence of such principles was a consequence of allowing 'illiterate mechanick persons' to engage in religious speculation (notwithstanding, of course, that the Levellers' leaders were far from illiterate!). More recent students of their writings, too, have tended to agree that Leveller views were not uninformed by religious ideas.

Certainly the main leaders of the movement had more than a passing interest in religion, Lilburne attesting to a powerful conversion to Christ in his youth when God 'washed and clensed my soul with the precious blood of Jesus Christ', and Overton drawing upon biblical texts such as 'I know my Redeemer liveth' and 'I know my life is hid in Christ' to express his own personal faith.

Overton and Walwyn both also wrote on religious themes in the early 1640s. And the Leveller leaders clearly also drew upon religious beliefs when shaping their political thought: Lilburne spoke of God 'engraving with his Spirit upon my heart' the golden rule, 'do unto others as you would have them do unto you', and this was not just a rule for Christians to follow, he argued, for God had engraved it on every heart with the intention that all should live by it. Indeed, Overton thought this rule the foundational principle which made civil society possible, and from it derives the Levellers' doctrine of equity.

Walwyn also saw Christianity as primarily a religion of the 'golden rule', and argued that the real measure of any doctrine was its usefulness. The essence of Christianity lay in 'universal love to all mankind without respect of persons, opinions, societies ... churches or forms of worship': love always led people to want to do good, and 'true Christians' were 'the most valiant defenders of the just liberties'. Walwyn denied being in fellowship with any sectaries, though he joined 'heart and hand with them in anything that I judge to be right and tending to the public good'. Overton's conflation of soul and body in *Mans Mortalitie*, a doctrine which served to weaken the Church's ability literally to put the fear of Hell into parishioners who stepped out of line, can be discerned underpinning his claim that 'to every individual in nature is given an individual property by nature, not to be usurped by any' – from which the core idea that all are born equal 'to like propriety, liberty and freedom' can be derived. There was not necessarily a contradiction in arguing for the essential rationality of human beings and the implanting of that rationality in them by God: God made each person 'naturally a rational creature, judging rightly all things and desiring only what was necessary' wrote Walwyn. For Overton, God was 'not a God of irrationality, and madness, or tyranny: therefore all God's communications are reasonable and just, and what is so, is of God'.

The strong individualism in Leveller thinking was also rooted in the Calvinistic Puritanism that some of the movement's leaders encountered in their youth, and, in varying degrees, subscribed to in later life. Calvinism stressed the importance of the individual's one-to-one relationship with God, a relationship which gave to that individual worth, value and dignity: and the doctrine of predestination spoke of the inherent equality of all, no one person meriting God's favour over another on account of status, wealth or birth. Thus both beliefs challenged traditional ideas about how power was to be gained, used and restrained, and could lead to calls for equality in political rights. Calvinism also threatened prelacy, for a person chosen by God and in communication with God needed no priest to mediate his or her relationship with the divine or 'explain' to them the Scriptures. Even if many Levellers had moved away from an orthodox Calvinism by the end of the 1640s, their debt to its central tenets was considerable.

Leveller ideas about toleration are also rooted in their conviction, which they shared with many of their contemporaries, that Old Testament patterns of government no longer had any validity in the Christian age. The traditional view, held by those who upheld the concept of a national church, was that practices found in the Old Testament were forerunners or 'shadows' of practices followed by the church – so circumcision prefigured baptism, and the state of Israel, the church. Thus as Israel had been governed by kings charged with maintaining holy living by compulsion, so the church had a similar task to ensure that true religion was adhered to in the present age. But to Levellers this link could not be maintained, since the church was essentially a voluntary assembly sustained by faith. Further, as Wildman put it rather directly at Putney, the Bible gives no indication 'what is fit to be done in civil matters'. It was but a short step to argue that church and state should now have different spheres of competence and that it was not the duty of the magistrate to compel or restrict in matters of religion.

The Levellers' position on religion was complex and changed over time, but they appear generally to have agreed that the essence of religion was 'practical', involving fulfilling the basic gospel imperative to help those in need as well as overcoming injustice. 'We should soon become practical Christians', wrote Walwyn in 1649, 'and take more pleasure in feeding the hungry, clothing the naked, visiting and comforting the sick, relieving the aged, weak and impotent, in delivering of prisoners, supporting of poor families, or in freeing a commonwealth from all tyrants.' Christianity is a religion of love, and 'love makes you no longer your own but God's servant'. The true Christian is known by 'his good works'. 'The great end wherefore God sent man into the world was, that he should do good in his generation', said Lilburne in 1649. 'It's the command of God', wrote John Wildman in *Truths triumph* (1648) 'that every man should seek the good of his neighbour.'

Leveller thinking on equity and the need for laws based on this principle would also have been informed by the experience of meeting and worshipping with gathered churches, from which much of their support was drawn. In marked contrast to the hierarchical and authoritarian character of the established Church, the sects and dissenting congregations among which the Levellers moved followed – as we have noticed in the case of Baptists – an essentially democratic pattern of government, with ministers being elected by the congregation rather than being appointed over their head, and paid by the voluntary contributions of members rather than the extraction of tithes. The gospel of 'free grace' preached in many of these churches also had 'democratic implications' since, as David Wootton has said, 'if sinners could be saved, it was impossible in this world to know who were the saints who should rule and who the reprobate who should obey'.[7] The sects also established themselves on the basis of covenants or contracts freely entered into, which Overton himself once commented reflected the practice of the early Christians. The Leveller leaders would also have witnessed at Baptist and other separatist meetings people who ordinarily would not have had a public voice being accorded the right to speak – some, of course, being women.

Further, the strong emphasis on individual rights in Leveller thinking was based not on an isolationist ethics, but a strongly communitarian one informed by their practical understanding of Christianity. 'I was not born for myself alone', wrote Overton in 1646, 'but for my neighbour as well, and I am resolved to discharge the trust which God hath reposed in me for the good of others.' 'No man is born for himself only', begins the *Manifestation* of 1649, drafted principally by Walwyn: we are 'obliged by the laws of nature ... of Christianity ... and of public society and government, to employ our endeavours for the advancement of a communitive happiness, or equal concernment to others as ourselves.'

Only by securing mass support for their programme could the Levellers hope to see it implemented, and they put much effort into making their ideas known, initially finding a ready hearing among opponents of the king. Their tactic of drawing up petitions did much to increase their reach and profile, and their claims to speak on behalf of many thousands of their fellow citizens were probably not exaggerations: their *Humble Petition of divers wel affected Persons inhabiting the City of London* of September 1648 was alleged to have had 40,000 signatures, and *The Remonstrance of Many Thousands of the Free People of England*, published exactly one year later, nearly 100,000. Many of these petitions were circulated by the gathered churches, and their subsequent presentation to Parliament became occasions for mass rallies – as did the funerals of leading Leveller figures such as Thomas Rainsborough in 1648 and the mutineer Robert Lockyer the following year.

Yet they struggled to sustain this interest throughout the 1640s. Much of their support was concentrated in London and, to a lesser extent, the home counties, and while many of the capital's traders and artisans may have shared their critique of the government, not all embraced their solutions or found their perceived lack of interest in economic change helpful in straitened times. In due course many of their followers in the gathered churches, including Baptists, decided to accommodate themselves to the new administration under Cromwell, and the Levellers alienated others of their natural supporters in these congregations by their espousal of a secular state and toleration for all. It was this failure to maintain the support of the godly 'middling sort', their real organizational power base, that was ultimately to prove decisive for their fortunes, given that their programme had little to commend it to the very rich or very poor.

Outside of the gathered churches Levellers worked hard to gain support among the army, a task that became easier after 1647 when the need for a political solution to the crisis surrounding the king became necessary and grievances over pay and conditions began causing dissent in the ranks. Among soldiers fearful that Parliament and the army generals were about to sell them out and betray the ideals for which they had risked their lives, their programme was well received, to the extent that the army was seen by some observers as 'one Lilburne throughout'; and by the summer, when the various regiments began electing 'agitators' to present their demands to the leadership, many of those chosen were Levellers. In the autumn, when their pamphlet *The Case of the Armie Truly Stated* gained acceptance by both 'agitators' and rank and file as a true statement of their grievances, Cromwell was sufficiently concerned to agree to a debate in Putney Church with the agitators and specially invited Leveller spokespeople.

These debates in October and November provided a unique opportunity for the Levellers to argue their case with the people who mattered: Cromwell and the other army grandees. The document on the table was the first 'Agreement of the People', a reworked version of *The Case of the Armie*, clearly setting out the case for a fairer distribution of parliamentary seats; religious toleration; an end to conscription; and equality under the law – there must be no discrimination with respect to the law on grounds of 'tenure, estate, charter, degree, birth or place'. According to the (admittedly incomplete) transcript of the debate compiled by the army secretary, William Clarke, the Levellers' demands were presented with skill and passion, not least by Rainsborough and Wildman (the main drafter of *The Case*); but the argument ultimately went the way of the chief speaker for the grandees, Henry Ireton, particularly in so far as he could demonstrate the inconsistency of the Levellers' position regarding the franchise and property. Ireton was not opposed to extending the franchise, and appears to have been party to a compromise formula which would have granted the vote to 'all soldiers and others, if they be not servants or beggars ... although they have not forty shillings per annum in freehold'. But, perhaps with a greater concern for political realities, he contended that if the Levellers upheld the principle of private property *and* argued for more men to be given the vote, then 'why may not those men vote against all property?'

After Putney, Leveller influence in the army declined. Their attempts to stir the troops to action failed, and a poorly planned mutiny at Corkbush Field near Ware in Hertfordshire in November was defused, Cromwell riding among the troops to remove copies of the 'Agreement' which were tucked in their hats. Although Cromwell and Ireton approached Lilburne again in November 1648 following the breakdown of their negotiations with the king, and Levellers and army leaders met for further debates at Whitehall in December and January, the settlement that year of the soldiers' grievances – which the Levellers had hitherto been able to exploit – seriously weakened their position. An army mutiny in London in April 1649, which resulted in the execution of Robert Lockyer, and further mutinies in May, gave the Levellers perhaps their last real chance for further negotiation, but the mutineers were successfully overcome by Cromwell during a stopover in Burford, and three Levellers – Cornet Thompson, Corporal Church and Private Perkins – executed outside the church. Levellers by and large felt betrayed by the new administration and by Cromwell, whose verdict on them – 'a despicable and contemptible generation of men', 'persons differing little from beasts' – suggests there was little love lost between them.

That the Levellers were a spent force by the end of the decade was underlined by the punishment inflicted on their leaders. In February 1649, following the publication of Lilburne's *England's New Chaines Discovered*, he, Walwyn, Overton and Prince were all committed to the Tower, and although they issued their third Agreement of the People during their captivity, their support was by then on the wane. Lilburne was arrested again in 1653, and, although acquitted, he was held for some time on the island of Jersey and subsequently detained in England until his death in 1657. Overton was also imprisoned again from 1655 until 1659. In

1654 Wildman worked with a few army leaders to produce a joint manifesto, *The Humble Petition of Several Colonels of the Army*, which mourned the fact that so many had fought to rid the country of the king, apparently for nothing. The title of a tract Wildman compiled in 1655, *A Declaration of the Free-Born People of England, Now in Armes Against the Tyrannie and Oppression of Oliver Cromwell, Esq,* perhaps summed up Leveller disillusionment with the new regime. Lilburne's trial in 1653 prompted demonstrations in London and some 20 new pamphlets, but by then many former Leveller supporters had come to think that even the return of monarchy might be better than the army.

So the Leveller movement flourished for at most six years. On one level its impact was small, none of its leaders living to see any of their major proposals established; and perhaps with hindsight we might conclude that the only way those proposals *could* have come into being was by the inherently contradictory manner of imposition. From the perspective of the political establishment their programme had essentially nothing to offer, and hence there was no prospect of it being realized by consent; and the Levellers themselves were unable to build sufficient support among the 'middling people', whose interests they especially represented, to build a mass movement for change, and failed to engage those lower down the social scale. Perhaps they also suffered because, finding their main support bases in the army and the Baptist churches, they pursued issues which were deeply unpopular with Parliament and on which, in the end, Cromwell out-manoeuvred them – namely a fair deal for the soldiery and religious toleration. Yet their key proposals – universal franchise, salaries for MPs, elimination of 'pocket boroughs', frequent parliaments, decentralization of power – far outlived the movement itself, and were not truly to have their day until the nineteenth century, when the Chartists gave them new life, and even later.

As David Wootton has argued in an important essay, it is hard for us, at this distance of time, to grasp how revolutionary the Levellers were: in seeking a written constitution based on inalienable natural rights and measures such as equality of all under the law, freedom of conscience, limitations on government power in accord with the principles of natural justice and voting rights for the poor, they 'were not merely seeking to establish in England freedoms that existed elsewhere ... but ... for the first time freedoms which (outside of a mythical historical past, that of Anglo-Saxon England) never had existed, and were not to come into existence for over three centuries.'[8] In a reflective passage in *England's New Chaines Discovered*, Lilburne talked of posterity which, 'we doubt not, shall reap the benefit of our labours, whatever shall become of us'; and today, almost everything for which he and the movement argued – and suffered – we take for granted. Perhaps it is no surprise that critics and admirers continue to acknowledge the far-sightedness of their programme, and that their championing of the basic rights of the individual and calls for a government fully accountable to the people continue to inspire politicians and activists in a way that they themselves could never have imagined.

CHAPTER THREE

Diggers

I F THE LEVELLERS never resolved the tension created by their commitment both to extend the franchise and maintain the right to property, the 'True Levellers' or Diggers faced no such dilemma. They were clear that merely giving more people the vote would not bring about the 'freedom' which Parliament had promised to those who had risked their lives fighting the king, nor would it end the hunger to which so many were still subject if the rich were allowed to continue parcelling off areas of land for themselves. What the 'poor oppressed people of England' needed was *economic* and not merely *political* freedom, the restoration of the land to communal ownership and the abolition of the concept of 'thine' and 'mine'. If the Leveller John Lilburne could argue that 'the poorest that lives hath as true a right to give a vote as well as the richest and greatest', for Diggers, 'the poorest man hath as true a title and just right to the land, as the richest man'.

Diggers saw political liberty to be inseparable from economic liberty, and they stood apart from most of their contemporaries in wanting to see the overthrow of monarchy consolidated in the establishment of a truly communitarian order. While many voices in the 1640s and 50s called for thoroughgoing religious and political change, few apart from the Diggers argued that, without a fundamental re-structuring of the pattern of land-ownership, no political or social change would be of the slightest benefit to the poor and dispossessed. Now that the king had gone, Diggers argued, Parliament must seize the opportunity to dismantle the whole inequitable system of private land-ownership over which he had presided, and restore the land to its rightful owners, the people. And not only did they plead for such a restoration, they took up their spades and began to cultivate the waste and common land, hoping to set in train the process of making the earth once more a 'common treasury' for all to enjoy.

The first account we have of the Diggers' activities is a note sent on 16 April 1649 by Henry Sanders, a yeoman of Walton upon Thames in Surrey, to the Council of State. The Sunday of the previous week, Sanders tells the Council, 'one Everard, once of the army but was cashiered, who termeth himself a prophet, one Stewer and Colten, and two more, all living at Cobham, came to St George's Hill in Surrey, and began to dig on that side of the Hill next to Campe Close, and sowed the ground with parsnips, and carrots, and beans.' On the Monday following, Sanders continues, they were there again in increased numbers; on the Tuesday they burnt at least 40 rood of heath, 'which is a very great prejudice to the town'; and on the Friday between 20 and 30 came again 'and wrought all day at digging'. 'They invite all to come in and help them, and promise them meat, drink and clothes', Sanders writes, noting with obvious concern their intention to open up and cultivate local parks and expectation that 'four or five thousand' will join them 'within ten days'. Sanders also claimed that the community of diggers planned to force local people to come and work with them, and had issued a warning that they would cut the legs off any cattle found straying near their plantation. 'It is feared they have some design in hand', Sanders ended darkly.

Sensing that the whole affair was probably 'ridiculous' but that things might nevertheless get out of hand, the Council instructed Lord General Thomas Fairfax to investigate the 'tumultuous sort of people assembling themselves together' on St George's Hill. Council members noted in particular the Hill's proximity to the former royal palace of Oatlands. However, in the opinion of Captain John Gladman, whom Fairfax sent to investigate the Diggers, the

Council's worries were misplaced: noting that he had met the two ringleaders, Gerrard Winstanley and William Everard, and that they had agreed to meet with Fairfax, Gladman concluded that 'the business is not worth the writing nor yet taking notice of: I wonder the Council of State should be so abused with informations.' Everard, Gladman averred, was 'no other than a mad man'.

An insight into what might have inspired Winstanley, Everard and their group to begin digging on St George's Hill can be gleaned from Winstanley's own writings. In a tract entitled *The New Law of Righteousnes*, published in the January, Winstanley explains his belief that poverty is rooted in the practice of 'buying and selling the earth from one particular hand to another': because some people have the right to say of the land, 'this is mine', others are prevented from seeking nourishment from it and are able to survive only by working for landlords 'for small wages'. It is 'as if the earth were made for a few, not all men', Winstanley writes. However, he adds, the days of such practice are numbered, and will end very shortly when Christ begins to rise in his people and lead them once more to act righteously toward one another.

Writing during the heady weeks leading up to the execution of Charles Stuart, and confronting widespread hunger and poverty occasioned by the worst run of bad harvests for more than a century, Winstanley is assured that 'it is the fullness of time' and that the 'restorer of the earth' will shortly 'make the earth a common treasury' once again. He also discerns a role for himself in bringing this about, receiving in a trance the words 'work together, eat bread together', and a warning that the hand of the Lord will be upon those who labour for those who call themselves 'lords and rulers' but are in fact their equals. Accordingly, Winstanley continues,

> *when the Lord doth shew unto me the place and manner,*
> *how he will have us that are called common people, to*
> *manure and work upon the common lands, I will then go*
> *forth and declare it in my action, to eat my bread with*

*the sweat of my brows, without either giving or taking
hire, looking upon the land as freely mine as another's.*

Within a few weeks the 'place and manner' had been confirmed,
and on Sunday the first (or possibly the eighth) of April the digging
began on St George's Hill.

As Sanders' representation to the Council of State implies,
Winstanley and his companions were not allowed to pursue their
digging in peace. Following the investigation by Gladman,
Winstanley and Everard duly met with Fairfax – declining to
remove their hats since the general was 'but their fellow creature' –
and informed him that they wanted to cultivate communally the
waste land which they now claimed rightfully belonged to the poor.
They assured him that they would not interfere with enclosed or
privately owned land but would 'meddle only with what was common and untilled'. The two men expressed their hope that many
others would shortly follow their example, and that all who owned
property would voluntarily give it up and join their communal
enterprise. They also undertook not to use force, even in self-
defence. Fairfax later visited the St George's Hill colony himself,
but despite his continued belief that the Diggers posed no threat to
the local populace, the latter maintained an aggressive posture
towards the community, several times subjecting its members and
their crops and houses to attack.

The first recorded invasion of the colony involved, as
Winstanley recorded it, 'divers of the diggers' being taken into the
village of Walton and locked in the church, later to be freed by a
justice of the peace. On another occasion some local freeholders,
dressed as women, staged a violent attack on the community.
Subsequently, following a change of tactic on the part of their
opponents, a group of Diggers, including Winstanley (but not
Everard, who appears to have left the community shortly after the
interview with Fairfax) were indicted for trespass at Kingston
Court and fined £10 each, with plaintiff's costs of 29s 1d (£1.46).
Since they were unable to pay these costs, their property was
sequestrated. Fairfax made another visit to the Hill in May, during
which Winstanley apparently informed him that, although his

group was digging upon crown lands, 'the king that possessed them by the Norman Conquest being dead, they were returned again to the common people of England, who might improve them if they would take the pains'. Several newspapers of the day took up the Diggers' story, but either misrepresented them – one paper described them as 'seekers' – or dismissed them as 'a company of crack-brains, which are digging out their own ruins'. *Mercurius Pragmaticus* ridiculed 'Prophet Everard's' intention to turn 'Oatlands Park into a wilderness and preach liberty to the oppressed deer', and warned its readers that 'what this fanatical insurrection may grow unto, cannot be conceived; for Mahomet had as small, and as despicable a beginning'.

The Diggers issued a number of tracts during their occupation of St George's Hill (or 'George Hill' as they preferred to call it, refusing to recognize the saints of the established Church). The first, *A Declaration to the Powers of England* (more commonly known as *The True Levellers Standard Advanced*), drafted by Winstanley though signed by Everard and 13 other named people, took the form of a manifesto, explaining that the purpose behind their work was to 'lay the foundation for making the earth a common treasury for all'. George Hill, they explained, was only the beginning, since

> *not only this common or heath should be taken in and*
> *manured by the people, but all the commons and waste*
> *ground in England, and in the whole world, shall be*
> *taken in by the people in righteousness, not owning any*
> *property; but taking the earth to be a common treasury,*
> *as it was first made for all.*

The community also set out its belief that all the prophecies and visions in Scripture pointing to the 'restoration of Israel', a time when all will enjoy once again the fruits of the earth and be freed from poverty and begging, centred upon the work of digging: this was the 'fulness of time' when the stench made by the hypocrisy of the priests and other 'powers of the world' would be overcome. In a second manifesto, *A Declaration from the Poor Oppressed People of England*, issued on 1 June, the Diggers asserted their right not only to the common land, but to 'the woods and trees that grow upon the commons' which they intended to cut down and sell until their crops were ready for consumption. They appealed to all wood-mongers not to buy their stock from those who felled 'our common woods and trees' for their own private gain, but from 'the poor'.

The publication of this second document provoked another violent attack on the Diggers, this time involving a garrison of soldiers stationed at Walton, and by August, having given up the struggle to survive at St George's Hill, the group moved a short distance to Cobham Heath and once more erected houses and planted grain. They announced the move in verse in their tract *A Watch-word to the City of London and the Armie* – 'In Cobham on the Little Heath our digging there goes on, / and all our friends they live in love, as if they were but one' – yet trouble eventually followed them there too. While the people of Cobham appear to have been much less hostile to the Diggers than the residents of Walton, and may have treated them with some respect, the lord of the manor, Parson John Platt, worked hard to turn the communities of nearby West Horsley (where he was rector) and Stoke d'Abernon against the colony. Platt eventually succeeded in getting the Diggers taken to court for riotous assembly, and further trouble ensued later in the year when the Council of State, alerted to the presence of 'a great number of persons gathered together about Cobham in a tumultuous and riotous manner', again sent Fairfax to intervene. The involvement of soldiers in attacks on his colony Winstanley attributed to the efforts of Platt, and in his *A New-yeers Gift for the Parliament and Armie*, published following the violent destruction of their houses, he appeared to sound the death knell for the digging experiment: 'I have writ, I have acted, I have peace', he writes towards the end of the tract, 'and now I must wait to see the Spirit do his own work in the hearts of others, and whether England shall be the first land, or some other, wherein Truth shall sit down in triumph.'

In fact the community struggled on, and in March 1650 several of its members, including Winstanley, signed the oath of loyalty to the republic, the 'Engagement', promulgated by the Rump Parliament. The Diggers also continued to publish tracts which implied that they still believed the venture could succeed, and in the spring the community appeared to find a new lease of life, building six or seven houses and cultivating some 11 acres of land. But just a few days after celebrating Easter, Parson Platt, despite pledging to leave the Diggers alone if Winstanley justified his actions from Scripture (which he had endeavoured to do), gathered some 50 men and violently crushed their settlement on the Heath. The Diggers' houses and other effects were all burned, and many were physically attacked, one woman being caused to miscarry.

Although the Diggers' message had begun to spread, with colonies being established as far afield as Wellingborough in Northamptonshire, Iver in Buckinghamshire, Barnet, Enfield and unidentified places in Kent, Gloucestershire and Nottinghamshire, Winstanley's hope to see all the commons and waste ground in England taken over by the poor oppressed people was not to materialize. In a symbolic winding-up of the Cobham venture, the Diggers took 20 of their oppressors to court for setting fire to their houses, only to see their case overturned, while proceedings against the Diggers themselves saw them indicted for riot, trespass and erecting cottages illegally on common land.

The Diggers' critique of the system of private land-ownership begins with the premise that the earth was originally created for all to share: 'In the beginning of time the great creator Reason made the earth to be a common treasury', they declare on the opening page of *The True Levellers Standard Advanced*. The concept of individual ownership of the land was not written into the creation narrative: originally, as Winstanley writes in *The Fire in the Bush* (1650), 'the whole earth was common to all without exception', with the more physically able helping the weaker by working harder, but the 'singleness and simplicity' of this arrangement became corrupted once the stronger began to argue their right to a larger share of the earth than the weaker. In a highly unorthodox way Winstanley understood this development, not as a consequence of the 'fall' of Adam, but the first step of the fall itself, and it was followed by the second, the 'outward action', in which the stronger physically appropriated land for themselves. 'The elder brother moves him to set about to enclose parcels of the earth into several divisions, and calls those enclosures proper or peculiar to himself, and that the younger or weaker brother should lay no claim to it, and the younger brother lets it go so …'.

Winstanley's employment of terms such as elder and younger brother reflect his conviction that the biblical narrative continues to be lived out in contemporary struggles between the rich and powerful and the poor and weak: Cain is still murdering Abel, Esau still seeking to secure Jacob's birthright, Ishmael still at odds with Isaac. Even more frequently Winstanley invokes 'Adam', who he argues should not be seen as 'a man … that disobeyed about 6000 years ago' but present now within every person. Adam is 'the first power that appears to act and rule in every man', he writes in the *New Law of Righteousnes*, and, like Esau, he gets the birthright which 'by the law of equity was more properly Jacob's'. But the point for Winstanley is that, just as Jacob in the end prevails, so the 'Adam' that dwells in each person will be overcome by the rising of the 'second Adam', 'the power of Christ', 'the Son bringing honour and peace': and 'this second man is the spiritual man, that judges all things according to the law of equity and reason'.

This struggle between two powers, 'flesh' and 'spirit', 'light and darkness', Winstanley observes both in society at large, as the rich subjugate the poor, and within every human being. But the older brother will not overcome indefinitely, for, 'in the fullness of time',

> When the first man hath filled the creation full of his
> filthiness, and all places stink with unrighteousness, as it
> doth at this day; then it pleaseth the Father, that his own
> wisdom and power should arise up next to rule in
> mankind in righteousness, and take the kingdom out of
> others' hand, and restore all things, and establish the

creation in peace, and declare himself to be the alone
Saviour of the world...

As Christopher Rowland and Jonathan Roberts point out, for Winstanley 'humanity, severally and corporately, stands in need of redemption' from the fall, from the practice of buying and selling the land; and while this will have a personal dimension – Christ the 'spiritual "man" in the life of individuals will overthrow the corrupt regime of the fleshly' – the 'Spiritual democracy' at the root of Winstanley's vision 'means that the redemption of the earth will necessarily be a communal event'.[1] As Winstanley writes,

> *When this universal law of equity rises up in every man*
> *and woman, then none shall lay claim to any creature*
> *and say, 'This is mine, and that is yours, This is my work,*
> *that is yours'; but every one shall put to their hands to till*
> *the earth, and bring up cattle, and the blessing of the*
> *earth shall be common to all.*

Violence will sometimes be a factor as the elder brother seeks dominance over the younger: as the Diggers tell the 'lords of manors' in their *Declaration from the Poor Oppressed People of England*, their (the lords') ancestors originally acquired their land by the sword, and 'first did murder their fellow creatures, men, and after plunder or steal away their land, and left this land successively to you, their children'. Winstanley also attributes the breakdown of the original 'communitarian' mode of existence to what he calls 'selfish imagination' taking 'possession of the five senses' and setting up 'one man to teach and rule over another'. Imagination, for Winstanley, is the feeling of incompleteness, fear and uncertainty which alienates people from the true knowledge of God or 'Reason', and the consequence of its appearance is that the earth, originally 'made a common store-house for all, is bought and sold, and kept in the hands of a few, whereby the great Creator is mightily dishonoured'.

It was of central importance to the Diggers, then, to see the earth once more restored to communal ownership, and in believing that this was possible they went further than most of their contemporaries. Conventional wisdom of the time was that, while a golden 'propertyless' age may once have existed, something innate in human nature made its realization again impossible: 'fallen' humankind had lost the state of innocence it once enjoyed in the Garden of Eden, and was now so subject to impulses of greed, fear, envy and lust that, for society to exist in any organized form, accommodation had to be made to the need to own and protect private property. Hence the concern of political philosophers was to construct the most workable social structures permitted by humanity's limitations and weaknesses – in the case of Winstanley's contemporary, Thomas Hobbes, for example, one where anarchy, the inevitable consequence of unbridled competitiveness, was held at bay only by a strong authoritative sovereign figure.

Winstanley, however, not only rejected the position Hobbes was soon to articulate in *Leviathan* – 'this ... power in man, that causes divisions and war is called by some men the state of nature, which every man brings into the world with him. But this law of darkness in the members is not the state of nature' he wrote in *Fire in the Bush* (1650) – but in a passage that remarkably anticipated much later thinking, actually suggests that human nature is largely shaped by the prevailing social conditions. 'I am assured that if it be rightly searched into', he writes in *The Law of Freedom* (1651), 'the inward bondages of the mind, as covetousness, hypocrisy, envy, sorrow, fears, desperation and madness, are all occasioned by the outward bondage that one sort of people lay upon another.' For Winstanley, there would be no need of laws or punishments once men and women had put an end to 'that cheating entanglement of buying and selling'.

Informed by his conviction that self-interest is not innate to men and women but generated and stimulated by the system of buying and selling – by Adam coming to rule in each person at the fall – Winstanley goes on to suggest, perhaps uniquely among his contemporaries, that the prelapsarian community might once again be attainable, once private property is abolished and Reason comes to reign once more in the human heart. His understanding of the fall as the introduction of private property, and not a separate state which gave rise to it, clearly informs his thinking, leading him to envisage a situation in which, as Reason once again holds sway, people embrace the idea of communitarian living as the only rational and just way to co-exist. The breakdown of the system of private ownership then becomes unstoppable.

For Diggers, of course, this was not just theory, and their name – given to them by the contemporary press though they seem to have preferred the name 'True Levellers' – originates from the method which they adopted to set off this process, breaking the ground with the spade. What the Diggers appear to have envisaged was a gradual process in which the common people in different localities, seeing the benefits of living communally, would follow their example and thereby bring about the disintegration of the system of hiring labour, the only way that the rich could manage their own huge estates. Their programme was effectively a call for a 'general strike' against landowners, and it sought to transform English society in the most radical way. As James Holstun has commented, 'the Diggers threatened the landed ruling class precisely because they inserted local knowledge into a national revolutionary project: preaching and publishing epistles to other disaffected tenants and wage laborers, to the Army, to Parliament, to London, to the universities; forming links among the scattered Digging communes; and developing a program for revolution based in a transformation of productive relations at the local level.'[2]

While the Diggers' action was inspired by their commitment to re-make the earth as a common treasury, and their sense that this was the propitious time for such a venture, they were also driven by the simple need to feed themselves and their dependants. The year in which the digging began came towards the end of one of the most serious depressions of the early modern period, with a run of bad harvests causing widespread poverty and starvation; and they allude to their poverty and want of 'bread to feed upon', and to the lords of the land seeing their 'fellow-creatures starve for want of bread, that have an equal right to it', in an early tract. An even more explicit statement appears in the Wellingborough Diggers' 'Declaration' of March 1650: 'we have spent all we have', they write,

> *our trading is decayed, our wives and children cry for*
> *bread, our lives are a burden to us, divers of us having 5,*
> *6, 7, 8, 9 in family, and we cannot get bread for one of*
> *them by labour; rich men's hearts are hardened, they will*
> *not give us if we beg at their doors; if we steal the law*
> *will end our lives, divers of the poor are starved to death*
> *already, and it were better for us that are living to die by*
> *the sword than by the famine.*

❦

Central to the Diggers' hopes for the restoration of society along communitarian lines was a belief that such a restoration embodied the second coming of Christ, the overpowering of the 'first Adam' by the second. For the Diggers, Christ was not expected to appear in some sudden or dramatic way 'in the clouds', or even as an individual person at all, but to 'rise up' in men and women, re-awaken them to the rule of Reason within them, and lead them to embrace the principle of community lost since the fall. From his earliest pre-Digger writings, Winstanley argued that Christ should be not understood as distinct from the saints, 'his body and spiritual house': 'Christ is not a single man at a distance from you', he wrote in *The Saints Paradice* (1648) but 'is the wisdom and power of the father, who spirits the whole creation, dwelling and ruling king of righteousness in your very flesh.' Thus he can equate the second coming with the gradual transformation of humanity.

In another unorthodox twist he also appears to see Christ's resurrection in the same light, even to conflate that event with his second coming: to expect Christ to 'come in one single person' is to 'mistake the resurrection of Christ … you must see, feel and know from himself his own resurrection within you'. But however

Winstanley understood Christ's return, its effect will be the restoration of true community or communism: as he wrote in *The New Law of Righteousnes* in January 1649,

> *when [Christ] hath spread himself abroad amongst his sons and daughters, the members of his mystical body, then this community of love and righteousness, making all to use the blessings of the earth as a common treasury amongst them, shall break forth again in his glory, and fill the earth, and shall be no more suppressed: and none shall say, this is mine, but every one shall preserve each other in love.*

Some commentators have seen the act of digging as largely symbolic, a 'signal' that the new age was dawning or that the Diggers were ready for God to transform society in some supernatural way, not an attempt to realize that transformation themselves. Now there *is* a sense in which Winstanley must have understood the fulfilment of his vision of England becoming a common treasury to be dependent upon some kind of divine intervention, because in purely *economic* terms it was unworkable: it would have required a large section of the population to be fed from land which had hitherto not been arable. Hence it is arguable that the Diggers sustained their commitment to their project in part because it had a theological and mystical dimension which identified the communization of the land with the lifting-up of the creation from bondage and restoration of all things from the curse. And Winstanley does also appear to have understood this lifting-up of the creation to embrace not only the regaining of a true spirit of community among men and women, but changes in the natural world and the return of the land to its prelapsarian fertile state:

> *When this restoration breaks forth in righteous action, the curse shall then be removed from the creation, fire, water, earth and air ... there shall be no barrenness in the earth or cattle, for they shall bring forth abundantly. Unseasonable storms of weather shall cease, for all the*

curse shall be removed from all, and every creature shall rejoice in righteousness one in another throughout the whole creation.

His fellow-Digger Robert Coster also alludes to a time when 'the corn will be green', store-houses will be filled and 'all things shall yield sweet increase' in his *A Mite Cast Into the Common Treasury*, published in December 1649.

There may also be significance in Winstanley's 'choice' of what appears to have been a particularly unpromising piece of common land to begin his project: one of his contemporary detractors, William Blith, commented that 'if there be not thousands of places more capable of improvement than theirs, and that by many easier ways, and to far greater advantage, I will lay down the bucklers', and Winstanley himself noted more than once that the soil he was digging on George Hill was 'very barren'. Yet his apparent expectation that divine assistance would help his cause should not obscure the fact that he also considered how *practically* he might realize his vision: believing that his programme coincided with the divine purpose did not preclude the necessity of working to bring that purpose about – in fact, quite the reverse, as his reflection at the beginning of *A Watch-word to the City of London* that 'action is the life of all, and if thou dost not act, thou dost nothing' makes clear. His assertion that the power that rises up in place of Adam, the 'second' or 'spiritual man', is 'not a talker, but an actor of righteousness', further underlines his commitment to action. Hence turning the soil and calling others to join them in their work had, for the Diggers, a far more than symbolic intent.

The Diggers took other practical steps to pursue their vision, including the employment of new agricultural techniques which were designed to make more of the land fertile. These included the planting of crops which could survive in dry and sandy soil, the use of those crops to maintain more animals and therefore produce more manure, and the pasturing of animals on land that would also be used, in rotation, for arable. The common land on which the Diggers operated was, after all, only common because its soil was poor and suitable mainly for grazing, whereas their attempts to work the soil would have gradually rendered land that had hitherto been infertile and unproductive suitable for growing corn and other 'staple' crops. And that there was enough land with the potential to become fertile Winstanley had also worked out: 'divide England into three parts', he wrote in *The New Law of Righteousnes*, 'scarce one part is manured: so that here is land enough to maintain all her children'.

Winstanley believed profoundly in the sacred quality of the land. This is implied in his 'immanentist' understanding of God or 'Reason', and also in so far as he imagines Christ still to be 'buried' in the earth, working for its good while awaiting the opportunity to rise in his sons and daughters (which, for Winstanley, is also his second coming). 'The body of Christ is where the Father is, in the earth, purifying the earth', he writes in one of his pre-Digger tracts, *Truth Lifting up his head above Scandals* (1648). The land is also crucial for Winstanley because it is the very source and sustainer of life: the earth is our 'Mother … that brought us all forth' and who, because of her love for us all, wants to give 'all her children suck … that they starve not', something she is hindered from doing all the while the landlords enclose off the land.

Winstanley appears to have held to a form of millenarianism throughout the digging and beyond. In his very first writing *The Mystery of God*, published in 1648 but possibly drafted some time before, he linked this to a 'dispensationalist' understanding of history, according to which the biblical narrative is divided into periods or dispensations, each marked at their beginning and end by an event of great religious significance, and each symbolic of the progressing and deepening relationship between God and God's creation. Winstanley discerned himself, like all millenarians, to be living in the penultimate phase of history, during which the elect 'are to be gathered into one city and perfected' in readiness for the final dispensation when the whole creation will be set free. If in his later writings his interest in dispensationalism appears to wane, he maintains a dependence upon the apocalyptic literature of the Bible to provide a key to understanding the signs of the times.

The imagery of the Beast or Serpent, representing those who oppose the work of the people of God, remains central to his thinking, and the biblical prophecies concerning its ultimate defeat continue to reassure Winstanley that his hope is not in vain. One of the most frequently cited biblical verses in his writings is Genesis 3.15 in which God, addressing the serpent who tempted Eve, promises to 'put enmity between thee and the woman, and between thy seed and her seed, he shall break thy head, and thou shalt bruise his heel'. The Beast also appears in *A Declaration from the Poor Oppressed People of England*, together with its enigmatic number '666', which Winstanley uses to suggest that Charles I is 'the last tyrannical power that shall reign' before 'people shall live freely in the enjoyment of the earth, without bringing the mark of the Beast in their hands'. Later Winstanley castigates Parson Platt and other violent opponents of the Diggers as men who 'do so powerfully act the image of the Beast'.

Winstanley finds further pointers to the imminence of the new age in the biblical allusions to a figurative period of 'a time, times, and dividing of time' during which 'the Lord ... gives this Beast a toleration to rule'. In Winstanley's day this period was widely understood to signify a period of three and a half 'years' (a year, two years and half a year), each consisting of 360 'prophetical days' or ordinary years; and therefore the combined period of three and a half prophetical years is equal to a total of 42 months or 1,260 days (or years), the period, according to Revelation 13.5, granted to the Beast to exercise his power. This schema encouraged some of Winstanley's contemporaries to argue that the downfall of the Beast must be imminent, given that he was a representation of the Pope whose rise to power could be dated to around AD 390–6. If Winstanley himself avoided setting any precise dates he was in no doubt that he was living in the penultimate age or dispensation, and in *The True Levellers Standard Advanced* asserted that 'the righteous Father suffered himself ... to be suppressed for a time, times and dividing of time, or for 42 months, or for three days and a half, which are all but one and the same term of time: and the world is now come to the half day.'

❧

The Diggers shared with many of their contemporaries an abhorrence of the teaching of the established Church: for Winstanley its whole theological system was oppressive for the ordinary people to whom it was preached, and he rejected it wholesale. The clergy encouraged belief in a God beyond the creation, which, although Winstanley rejected on the grounds that such knowledge was 'beyond the line, or capacity of man to attain to while he lives in his compound body', he did the more so because he saw how the clergy contrived to make God appear punitive and capricious; this was the God who approved the unfair distribution of the earth originally given as a common treasury, and, significantly, 'who appointed the people to pay tithes to the clergy'. Both God and Christ, Winstanley considered, were held by the priests 'at-a-distance' so that they could then be mediated to the people only through them.

In addition the clergy fostered 'Imagination' in their hearers by preaching a historic 'fall' and emphasizing each individual's sinfulness, and as the people sought to reclaim their identity by relating to the God- and Christ-at-a-distance, so the clergy made them even more dependent upon themselves. With the addition of a heaven in the next life as reward for their subservience to them, or hell as a punishment for insubordination, the system by which the clergy reinforced their authority and power over the people was, for Winstanley, complete. 'By this divined hell after death', he wrote in *The Law of Freedom in a Platform*, 'they preach to keep both king and people in awe to them.' The clergy persuaded the people to think 'that true freedom lay in hearing them preach, and to enjoy that heaven which they say every man who believes their doctrine shall enjoy after he is dead: and so tell of a heaven and hell after death, which neither they nor we know what will be ...'.

In place of this alienating form of religion Winstanley stressed the immanence of God, who could be known by all without the 'aid' of the professional beneficed clergy. Humankind, he taught, need not be bowed down by Imagination: 'every single man, male and female, is a perfect creature of himself' and has the creator dwelling in him 'to be his teacher and ruler within himself'. Each person can therefore judge all things by experience, which is more important than the whole edifice of doctrine and church government built up on biblical texts and drawn from what he calls 'book-learning'. For Winstanley, heaven and hell are present states: heaven is humankind, and hell describes the conditions men and women have created for themselves on earth. Winstanley left open the question whether there may be a physical heaven or hell, but did hold the unorthodox (and under the 1648 Blasphemy Act, illegal) belief that all humanity would be saved.

Winstanley's use of the term 'Reason' for God emphasized God's immanence and contrasted sharply with that Imagination from which God would redeem 'sons and daughters' as Christ rose in them and brought them together again into community. 'I am made to change the name of God to Reason', he wrote in *Truth Lifting up his Head above Scandals*, 'because I have been held under darkness by that word as I see many people are.' The question of any antithesis between immanence and transcendence appears not to have concerned him: 'the same spirit that made the globe' is, for Winstanley, 'the indweller in the five senses of hearing, seeing, tasting, smelling and feeling'.

Like many other 'radicals' the Diggers had no time for the established clergy, whom they saw, along with landlords and lawyers, as an 'unholy trinity' upholding the present iniquitous system. But whereas many of their contemporaries were content to attack these groups individually, the Diggers developed a coherent analysis of their inter-connectedness, what Marxist political theorists might want to term their 'shared class interest'. The strongest hint of this is to be found in Winstanley's concept of 'kingly power', a collective term he employs for those institutions which together maintained the economic system which he perceived to be burdening the poor of his day. The term 'kingly' acknowledged not only that it was the monarch himself who was the 'figurehead' of the established order, but the role of William the Conqueror in uniting under him its various components.

The English legal system, Winstanley was clear, was introduced by William to reinforce the division of land he effected in 1066 in the interest of his lieutenants, and had been used by successive monarchs to their benefit ever since: 'law is but the strength, life and marrow of the kingly power' he wrote in *A*

New-yeers Gift, 'upholding the conquest still, hedging some into the earth, hedging out others ... truly most laws are but to enslave the poor to the rich.' Then, to ensure the enforcement of his laws, William appointed two 'national officers', the lawyer, whose 'work is conversant about nothing but the disposing of the earth', and the clergy, whose duty 'was to persuade the multitude of people to let William the Conqueror alone with a quiet possession and government of the earth, and to call it his and not theirs, and so not to rebel against him.' For their efforts in 'preaching for him' and bewitching the people into 'receiv[ing] him to be God's anointed over them', William rewarded the clergy by introducing a system of tithes requiring payment by the people of a tenth of their income to the Church. And 'if the clergy can get tithes or money, they will turn as the ruling power turns, any way'!

In *The Fire in the Bush* Winstanley also employs apocalyptic imagery to link clergy, landlords and lawyers, identifying the four beasts which Daniel saw rise out of the sea as 'kingly power', 'selfish laws', 'the thieving art of buying and selling the earth with her fruits to one another' and 'the imaginary clergy-power'. And although these appear to flourish for a time, oppressing and burdening the creation, they will 'run into the sea again, and be swallowed up in those waters; that is, into mankind, who shall be abundantly enlightened' at the glorious appearance of Christ.

The concept of 'kingly power' played a vital role in shaping Winstanley's response to the civil war. While he welcomed the removal of the monarchy and the Lords, he recognized that in themselves these developments would not be sufficient to lift the people's burden: kingly power was not in the hands of the king alone, but in those of the landlords, the lawyers and the 'tithing-priests'. With the execution of Charles, he argued, the 'top-bow is lopped off the tree of tyranny, and kingly power in that one particular is cast out; but alas oppression is a great tree still, and keeps off the sun of freedom from the poor commons still, he hath many branches and great roots which must be grubbed up, before every one can sing Sion's songs in peace'. The Diggers' solution, informed by their memory of Parliament's promise of freedom to the people in return for fighting the king, was straightforward, and they laid it out in their *A New-yeers-Gift for the Parliament and Armie*:

> *You have taken away the king; you have taken away the House of Lords: now step two steps further, and take away the power of lords of manors, and of tithing priests, and the intolerable oppressions of judges, by whom laws are corrupted; and your work will be honourable.*

'True religion, and undefiled', Winstanley wrote, summarizing his position in the last month of the digging,

> *is this, to make restitution of the earth, which hath been taken and held from the common people by the power of conquests formerly, and so set the oppressed free. Do not all strive to enjoy the land? The gentry strive for land, the clergy strive for land, the common people strive for land; and buying and selling is an art, whereby people endeavour to cheat one another of the land. Now if any can prove, from the law of righteousness, that the land was made peculiar to him and his successively, shutting others out, he shall enjoy it freely, for my part: but I affirm, it was made for all; and true religion is to let every one enjoy it.*

While the Diggers sought to advance their cause by petitioning Parliament and the army leadership, and by direct action in the form of digging, they never advocated the use of violence, despite being themselves subjected to it by their opponents. While some of their language might have been interpreted as threatening, particularly that directed against those whom they saw as the oppressors of the poor, they set out in *The True Levellers Standard Advanced* that 'there is no intent of tumult or fighting, but only to get bread to

70

eat, with the sweat of our brows; working together in righteousness, and eating the blessings of the earth in peace'.

In one sense, of course, armed struggle would hardly have been
a sensible option for such a tiny movement, but they also shared a
conviction that true freedom could not be obtained by means which
actually ended up enslaving people: resort to the sword would simply result in one section of society lording it over the other, as was
the case at present. 'We abhor fighting for freedom', they wrote in
A New-yeers Gift,

> *it is acting of the curse and lifting him higher; and do*
> *thou uphold it by the sword, we will not; we will*
> *conquer by love and patience, or else we count it no*
> *freedom: freedom gotten by the sword is an established*
> *bondage to some part or other of the creation ... victory*
> *that is gotten by the sword is a victory that slaves get one*
> *over another.*

Their belief in the *legality* of their cause also ruled out any consid-
eration of violence, since Parliament simply needed to recognize
that the execution of Charles had undermined the basis of his pred-
ecessor William's legislation enshrining property and had restored
again the people's right to the land. Further, if Christ was now rising in men and women to make the earth once more a common
treasury, this would be both a peaceful and unstoppable process.

Winstanley appears to have been resigned to the fact that the
Diggers' project would attract opposition and ridicule, but that
their 'foolishness' (in the eyes of their fellow men and women)
would prevail by virtue of its integrity. In a striking passage in *A
Watch-word to the city of London* Winstanley tells his influential
readers that, while they have stood for and prayed for freedom,
kept fast days, given thanks for victories and promised the people
freedom, they cannot bear to face the truth with which the Diggers
are confronting them:

> *now the common enemy is gone, you are all like men in a*
> *mist, seeking for freedom, and know not where, nor*

> *what it is: and those of the richer sort of you that see it*
> *are ashamed and afraid to own it, because it comes*
> *clothed in a clownish garment, and open to the best*
> *language that scoffing Ishmael can afford, or that railing*
> *Rabsheka can speak, or furious Pharaoh can act against*
> *him; for freedom is the man that will turn the world*
> *upside down, therefore no wonder he hath enemies.*

Even after the defeat of the digging venture Winstanley did not lose faith in the power of persuasion, and in his final work, *The Law of Freedom in a Platform*, entrusts responsibility for the realization of the blueprint for a new society that it contains to Cromwell: 'And now I have set a candle at your door', he tells the general, 'for you have power in your hand, in this other added opportunity, to act for common freedom if you will; I have no power.'

Following the violent termination of the digging at Cobham, the Digger community at Iver published a *Declaration* in May 1650, and its similarity to Winstanley's own writings suggests that he may have had a hand in its drafting. But while that is speculation, we do know that by harvest-time that year he was working on the estate of the prophetess Lady Eleanor Davies (sometimes Douglas) in Pirton in Hertfordshire, and that from 1652 he reintegrated himself into Cobham society, having originally settled there in 1643 following the collapse of his business in London, where he had been a freeman of the Merchant Taylors' Company. Like a number of other former Diggers, Winstanley held several parochial offices in the town in the late 1650s and 1660s, including churchwarden, though towards the end of his life he began attending Quaker meetings, with his second wife Elizabeth, and was buried as a Quaker in September 1676.

It is possible that Winstanley had had earlier links with the Friends, since Quakers and Diggers were often confused by contemporaries, and more than one writer in the seventeenth century considered Winstanley to have actually founded the Quakers. In 1654

Edward Burrough informed fellow Quaker Margaret Fell that 'Wilstandley says he believes we are sent to perfect that work which fell in their hands; he hath been with us.' If Winstanley's move to embrace Quaker doctrines appears broadly consistent with what we know of his convictions as a Digger, his apparent conformity to the established Church for a period, together with his involvement in legal proceedings concerning the estate of his recently deceased brother-in-law, from perhaps as early as 1652, raise interesting questions about his response to the summary ending of his venture at George Hill and Cobham, and his later attitudes to the institutions which he understood to constitute 'kingly power'.

Winstanley's only post-Digger writing, *The Law of Freedom in a Platform, or, True Magistracy Restored*, was dedicated to Cromwell in November 1651, though in its Dedicatory Epistle he implies that it had been drafted some two years previously. In this work Winstanley describes the new order he desires to see arise from the ashes of the old 'kingly government', one in which the earth is tilled in common and in which food and commodities are available for collection from storehouses without the need for money. In some respects this new society reflects that described in Thomas More's *Utopia*, though Winstanley never admits to using any source for his ideas other than Scripture. The importance of the family as the primary unit of society is stressed – the Diggers had always been keen to maintain that, unlike Ranters, they did not extend their commitment to common ownership to spouses – and both the system of law and the means for its enforcement are spelt out in considerable detail. Particularly noteworthy are the offences for which the death penalty will be invoked: buying and selling the land; practising law for money; preaching and praying for hire; homicide; and rape. That Winstanley perceives the need for a strong system of law and order in his new society suggests that he saw the process of Christ 'rising' in men and women, their reawakening to the rule of Reason within, occurring gradually. As he had maintained in his earlier writings, only when the practice of buying and selling finally disappears will there be no need of government or laws.

As John Gurney – who among present-day scholars has done more than most to shed new light on the Diggers and their impact –

has written, if Winstanley was correct in claiming that *The Law of Freedom* was drafted during 1649 or 1650, it 'can help us better understand the kind of social arrangements, and means of production and distribution, that he may have envisaged for Digger communities had they spread as successfully as he had hoped'.[3] That these communities did not spread, or even survive, leaves us with one of the great unknowns of history, namely how far the Diggers' call to the 'poor, oppressed people of England' to join them in remaking the earth as a 'common treasury' might have transformed the pattern of land ownership in England and beyond.

CHAPTER FOUR

Ranters

'A LL THE WORLD now is in the Ranting humour', wrote the author of *The Joviall-Crew, or the Devill turn'd Ranter*, a short play published in 1651. It was an exaggeration, of course, but it might have seemed to many right-thinking folk of the time that these devilish people whom they knew as Ranters were about to bring society to its knees. There may be parallels with how punks were received in the 1970s, or hippies the decade before.

To talk of Ranters making an impact in seventeenth-century England is not to suggest that there was any sort of movement by that name. In a culture which did not understand words such as 'sect' or 'party' in the tight, circumscribed way we do today, Ranters were an even more loose body of people than most. A book published in the 1980s even suggested that Ranters were no more than an invention of their contemporaries (and, indeed, of twenti-eth-century historians); the argument was that people such as Baptists and Quakers needed an 'image' on which to project all their fears of social and religious deviance, their temptations toward atheism and sexual misconduct, and so 'Ranters', a bit like witches, performed a social function as victims. Yet if 'Ranter' was a term of abuse foisted unwillingly on people, this was also true of labels given to Levellers and Quakers; but, more importantly, as with these other movements, we have sufficient independent evidence to enable us to arrive at some sort of understanding of what people meant when they used the term 'Ranter' – and a large number of people *did* use it.

When a parliamentary committee convened in 1650 to consider this new phenomenon, they spoke of 'a sect called Ranters'; and although 'sect' did not mean then what it has come to mean now the use of the term does imply some sort of 'collectivity' and shared understanding of what the nomenclature represented. Muggletonians also spoke of Ranters as a sect, and, like Quakers, used the term 'Ranter' as a stick with which to beat their opponents: an odd practice if Ranters did not actually exist. We may well conclude that there was no 'Ranter' movement, and certainly no leaders or formal 'membership' of any kind, but, as Jerome Friedman has argued on the basis of a careful study of the work of individual Ranters, 'despite significant differences, it would appear that Ranters recognized one another and the common core of views that each expressed'.[1]

Tom Corns, Professor of English at the University of Wales, has also noted how people described as Ranters had some sense of affinity with each other: Joseph Salmon sought out Abiezer Coppe when both ended up in the same gaol, and Coppe wrote in apparently intimate terms to Salmon; Lawrence Clarkson mentions fraternizing with Coppe and his circle; and Salmon clearly knew Jacob Bauthumley and sensed that they shared the same concerns. 'Perhaps not a movement', Corns realistically concludes, 'and indeed the persecution meted out to Coppe, Salmon and Bauthumley indicates a political climate in which such a movement would scarcely have survived; nevertheless, we may identify a looser configuration of mutual interests and sometimes compassion within a section of the radical milieu of 1649–51.'[2]

Ranters emerged mostly from the ranks of the Baptists, though they also had strong connections with people known as Seekers. An even more disparate grouping than Ranters, in that there survive no statements of their faith or guides to their practices, Seekers held that no church in existence exhibited the gifts or grace given by Christ to the apostles, and therefore the true believer should withdraw from formal worship and partaking of the sacraments. To their critics

Seekers were social misfits who, as one London preacher put it in 1644, whiled away their Sabbaths 'peeping in at church-doors, and taking essay of a sentence or two, and then if there be no scratch for [their] itch', disappearing. But Seekers themselves claimed to believe that all forms of visible church were apostate and thus it was necessary to wait patiently for the Holy Spirit to bring in a new, and proper, dispensation. 'To be solitary and walk alone is a wilderness condition, which with God is the most comfortable state', wrote William Erbery, described in 1646 as 'the champion of the Seekers' (though at other times as 'a loose person or a Ranter'); 'in that apostasy we now are, we cannot company with men, no not with saints, in spiritual worship but we shall commit spiritual whoredom with them.' Erbery was apparently not entirely uncomfortable with the accusation against him of Ranterism, though he refused to condone 'those profane people called Ranters' who blasphemed, cursed, whored and openly rejoiced in their wickedness.

One of the most difficult and challenging aspects of Ranter study, as John Carey has put it, 'is the disentangling of what these remarkable individuals actually thought and felt, not only from the misrepresentations of their enemies, but also from the confusion of their own writing'.[3] To an extent this is a problem with many of the individuals and groups of the mid-seventeenth century, but it seems even more so with people as extreme and unconventional as the Ranters. Yet we might start by asking what it is possible to glean from the (generally hostile) comments of their detractors and from their own small and (often abstruse) literary output.

One of the many who committed his concerns to print was John Bunyan, who relates in his *Grace Abounding to the Chief of Sinners* how, 'being but a young man, and my nature in its prime', he was tempted by some Ranters who told him 'that they only had attained to perfection that could do what they would, and not sin'. Bunyan tells how he lost an intimate companion to the Ranters, and how this man turned to 'cursing, and swearing and whoring' and would 'deny that there was a God, angel or spirit; and would laugh at all exhortations to sobriety'. Bunyan's attempts to confront this friend with his perilous eternal state were met with scorn: 'What would the devil do for company, if it were not for such as I am?'

Lodowicke Muggleton tells us that he and his cousin John Reeve encountered Ranters in London who told them that 'their God they worshipped was damned with them; for they had no other God but a spirit without a body, which they said was the life of every thing. So that the life of a dog, cat, toad, or any venomous beast, was the life of God: nay, that God was in a table, chair, or stool.' Having been commissioned by God as the Two Last Witnesses described in the book of Revelation, and given the authority to bless or damn friends and opponents to eternity, Muggleton and Reeve damned these Ranters, who in return tried to bribe three other men with 'a good dinner of pork' to curse *them*!

The Quaker leader George Fox records several encounters with groups of Ranters, noting their rudeness, their propensity to interrupt his preaching by singing, whistling and dancing, and their public boasting of and 'glorying in' their fornication. Fox tells how some Ranters in Reading tried to persuade him that God created the Devil. Richard Baxter was similarly unimpressed by Ranters, who 'spake the most hideous words of blasphemy, and many of them committed whoredoms commonly'. Their 'horrid villainies did as much as anything did, to disgrace all sectaries', he considered. Gerrard Winstanley devoted a whole tract to distancing his Digger community from 'Ranting', expressing his concern about their 'unreasonableness, madness and confusion', their 'excessive copulation with women', their 'idleness', their 'superabundant eating and drinking, which is the wasteful spending of the treasures of the earth', and their outward and abundant enjoyment of the 'five senses'.

One of Winstanley's concerns was to stress that his views on common ownership did not extend to spouses, but Ranters appear to have had no such qualms. A hostile tract published in 1650 noted the Ranters' belief that 'all women ought to be in common', and described how

> *when they assembled together ... with horrid oaths and*
> *execrations, then they fall to bowzing and drink deep*

healths ... to their brother God, and their brother Devil;
then being well heated with liquor, each brother takes
his she other upon his knee, and the word (spoken in
derision of the sacred writ) being given, viz, increase and
multiply, they fall to their lascivious embraces, with a
joint motion ...

Lawrence Clarkson admitted in *The Lost Sheep Found* (1660) that passages from the Song of Solomon were used as a ritual invocation in Ranter orgies.

A critic of Abiezer Coppe, perhaps the best known of the Ranters, noted how he would 'preach stark naked many blasphemies and unheard of villanies in the day-time, and in the night [get] drunk and lie with a wench, that had also been his hearer, stark naked'. (One wonders, of course, how such detail was obtained.) Another report noted how, 'when he was fitter to have gone to bed and slept, than to have spoken in a public place' Coppe 'bestowed an hour's time in belching forth imprecations, curses, and other such like stuff ... and when he perceived that he should be called to answer ... he took two of his she-disciples, and went to the city of Coventry, where it was soon dispersed abroad, that he commonly lay in bed with two women at a time.'

A less aggressive and more measured assessment of the Ranters appears in John Holland's *The Smoke of the Bottomless Pit* (1650). Both Christopher Hill and Nigel Smith (the latter the editor of a collection of Ranter writings) suggest that Holland gives a fairly accurate, if unsympathetic, account of what Ranter writings themselves say: Holland accuses Ranters of believing, Smith says,

that God is in man and in every creature, and that there
is one spirit in the world: good and bad spirits are
imaginary, while there is no sin since God has made it.
Thus, the Devil is the left hand of God, and there is no
heaven and hell but what is in man. The Scriptures and
Biblical commandments are rejected as contradictory,
and church ordinances are denied. Christ is a form or
shadow only of a transcendent truth, and what he did

in the flesh is now inside men in the spirit. Marriage is
seen as a curse, and there should be a complete liberty for
all to choose sexual partners.[4]

The West Country Baptist Thomas Collier summed up what he took to be Ranter (and for that matter Quaker) beliefs as 'no law but their lusts, no heaven nor glory but here, no sin but what men fancied to be so, no condemnation for sin but in the consciences of ignorant ones'.

The picture becomes even cloudier when taking into account works which have the appearance of being 'authentic' Ranter writings but which could also be 'black propaganda' circulated by their enemies. The anonymous *Justification of the Mad Crew*, for example, sets out clearly some of the heresies and practices which were frequently attributed to Coppe and other Ranters, but these positions Coppe went to great lengths to deny, and the pamphlet's explicit and overtly blasphemous tone point strongly to it being the work of an opponent wanting to set the Ranters up. On the other hand its title suggests that it could be the work of one or more Ranters or sympathizers wanting to be explicit about their beliefs, while, in perhaps a naive attempt to pre-empt their detractors, portraying themselves as 'fools'. In examining this work Corns has noted resonances between its frequent references to the term used in Genesis for carnal knowledge, becoming 'one flesh', and a group Lawrence Clarkson describes having visited in London called 'My One Flesh'; and this, as Corns says, raises interesting possibilities about its authorship. Some indication of the character of the London group may be gleaned from Clarkson's claim that he gained access to it by asserting that 'till you can lie with all women as one woman, and not judge it sin, you can do nothing but sin' – and to have found ample opportunity to prove its truth with female members of the group.[5]

'There is no sin': this was an article of faith for Ranters, who held that the Mosaic law was no longer binding upon true believers such as themselves. While many of their contemporaries, including Baptists, were 'antinomian' in the sense that they saw the gospel in terms of an unconditional gift from God rather than a law that carried obligations and required obedience on the part of the believer, they nevertheless believed that they should continue to obey the law as evidence of their faith. Ranters, however, took the extreme line that, if God indwelt a person, it was impossible for that person to commit sin and the law was therefore irrelevant.

The roots of their extreme antinomianism lay in their strong mystical and pantheist convictions: for Ranters, God had not only created all things but was present in everyone and every living thing; there was no God other than the one who indwelt the creation, 'man and beast, fish and fowl, and every green thing, from the highest cedar to the ivy on the wall', as Jacob Bauthumley put it. God does not exist outside the creatures: God is in 'this dog, this tobacco pipe, he is me and I am him'. The only difference in status between humankind and other objects of creation was the *extent* to which God was manifest in each. Only a few Ranters took this to the extreme of claiming actually to *be* God, but many did reach the conclusion that, since all their acts were prompted by God within, it was impossible for them to sin. Sin, if it existed, must be part of God's plan. 'A man as man hath no more power or freedom of will to do evil than he hath to do good', said Bauthumley; or as Richard Coppin (who denied being a Ranter but whose *Divine Teachings* was read by them) argued, the 'spiritual man can be no less than God, who is in all things', and therefore, like God, perfect, for 'where he is he is perfect; and in whom he is, he is perfect ...'. Seeing men and women as identical with the beasts, which is what Clarkson thought the writer of Ecclesiastes meant when saying that the fate of humans and animals was the same in that both returned to dust (3.19–20), gave some Ranters a perfect licence for unrestricted behaviour.

Sin, then, was entirely imaginary, a human creation, for, as Lawrence Clarkson argued, 'God made all things good ... [and] ... there was no such thing as theft, cheat or a lie, but as man made it so.' 'What act soever is done by thee in light and love, is light and lovely, though it be that act called adultery ... No matter what

Scripture, saints or churches say, if that within thee do not condemn thee, thou shalt not be condemned.' 'For sin', wrote Bauthumley, 'I cannot tell how to call it any thing, because it is nothing: I cannot give it a name, because it has no substance or creature.' Bauthumley agreed that people should be guided by the mind of God within them, not the Bible without: 'The sin lies not in these outward acts, for a man may do the self-same act, and yet not sin; that is, that a man drinks to excess, there is the sin, that a man drinks for necessity or delight, the same act and posture of body is put in the one, as the other.' Yet Bauthumley also had a high view of Scripture, seeing the Bible as 'the truest testimony of God in the world'.

One hostile pamphlet poked fun at Ranters' denial of sin, claiming that

> *they taught that they could neither see evil, know evil, nor act evil, and that whatsoever they did was good and not evil, there being no such thing as sin in the world. Whereupon Mistress E.B., striking fire at a tinder-box, lights up a candle, seeks under the bed, tables and stools, and at last coming to one of the men, she offers to unbutton his cod-piece; who demanding of her what she sought for? She answereth, For sin: whereupon he blows out the candle, leads her to bed, where in sight of all the rest, they commit fornication.*

Richard Baxter thought that Ranters lived by the text 'to the pure all things are pure', but took it as a licence for blasphemy and fornication. They believed that God looked not on the outward actions but on the heart.

Some Ranters thought that, since God created all things, even the Devil could be cleared of all the crimes for which he had been held responsible. In fact, however, there was little place in their highly unorthodox theology for any concept of Satan, hell, damnation, heaven or salvation: there could be no Devil, Bauthumley argued, for 'there is nothing hath a being but God'; heaven could not be 'any local place, because God is not confined'; and the Trinity was but a 'mystery of iniquity' since there was 'nothing in

Scripture or reason to countenance such a gross and carnal conceit of God'.

The Ranters' so-called Christmas Carol fuses their materialism, pantheism and profound impatience with orthodox beliefs:

> *They prate of God! Believe it, fellow-creatures,*
> > *There's no such bug-bear: all was made by Nature.*
> *We know all came out of nothing, and shall pass*
> > *Into the same condition once it was*
> *By Nature's power and that they grossly lie*
> > *That say there's hope of immortality,*
> *Let them but tell us what a soul is; then*
> > *We shall adhere to these mad brainsick men!*

To emphasize their unity with other human beings and the whole creation, Ranters used the words 'my fellow creature' as a salutation.

৩৽৶৶

It was not so much these beliefs themselves which shocked the Ranters' contemporaries, but the extreme way in which they interpreted them and their obvious readiness to act them out. They were, after all, hardly novel. Thomas Edwards' *Gangraena*, published in 1646, is full of people behaving and speaking as Ranters did, and many of their core doctrines had also caused concern when articulated by others earlier in the century. One hostile report notes extreme antinomian ideas circulating in the Yorkshire parish of Grindleton in 1617, where the curate, Roger Brearley, and his flock allegedly held that 'the Christian assured can never commit gross sin' and 'must never think of salvation'. If Grindletonians held anything to be sinful, the report suggested, it was asking God's forgiveness or believing the Word 'without a motion of the spirit'. The hyper-critical *Ranters Bible* links Ranters with the Family of Love – who believed in imitating Christ as closely as possible and in the possibility of divination as Christ entered the soul of the true follower – and the early heresy of Donatism, though 'Familism', to

83

which Grindletonians were also linked, was a term of abuse applied generally to extreme antinomian groups.

The point was that Ranters took everything to extremes, their behaviour the *reductio ad absurdum* of antinomianism. Reports by their detractors positively ooze with tales of their sexual immorality, drunkenness and blasphemy – to the extent, as Christopher Hill wryly notes, that the counter-attack was almost as threatening to orthodoxy as anything the Ranters themselves wrote![6] Operating on the premise 'till acted that so called sin, thou art not delivered from the power of sin', Ranters found ample opportunity to indulge their particular calling. For Lawrence Clarkson it was adultery, and, as we have noted, there seems to have been no shortage of women anxious for his services. He even received payment for providing them, which, he claimed, he was 'careful' to keep for his wife, who was presumably also grateful for his assurance that 'only my body was given to other women'. 'I can if it be my will, kiss and hug ladies and love my neighbour's wife as myself, without sin', Abiezer Coppe once said.

Ranter behaviour was overtly sacrilegious: the critical publication *Strange Newes from Newgate and the Old-Baily* (1651) opens with an account of how, while at dinner, one of a group of Ranters took a piece of beef in his hand and, 'tearing it asunder said to the other, This is the flesh of Christ, take and eat', while another 'took a cup of ale and threw it into the chimney corner, saying, There is the blood of Christ. And having some discourse of God it was proved that one of them said, That he could go into the house of office, and make a God every morning, by easing his body.' Ranters also used oaths profusely and offensively: Bulstrode Whitelocke reports hearing Joseph Salmon engage in 'wicked swearing and uncleanness' when he began preaching in Coventry, and Coppe, who was alleged to have once sworn for an hour on end in the pulpit, said he would 'rather hear a mighty angel (in man) swearing a full-mouthed oath, and see the spirit of Nehemiah (in any form of man, or woman) … making others fall a swearing, then hear a zealous [minister] pray, preach or exercise'.

Both Coppe and Salmon attributed their language to the God in them: swearing cannot be a sin if it is a divine voice doing the speaking. Hence Coppe can claim that 'God hath so cleared cursing, swearing, in some, that that which goes for swearing and cursing in them, is more glorious than praying and preaching in others.' And the Ranters' practice of swearing while preaching, though doubly offensive to many of their hearers, would presumably have been understood as an attempt to parody more orthodox behaviour: since Coppe can make full use of biblical allusions and references in his writings, he may well have done so in the pulpit. Swearing was part and parcel of Ranters' attempts to demonstrate how one could break free from all conventions. Salmon on one occasion describes his writing as 'the foolish language of the Spirit'.

കൈ

The behaviour of the Ranters might have been tolerated in times of peace, but in the explosive atmosphere of the 1650s the authorities thought it necessary to rein it in. Parliament considered both their beliefs and actions rendered them a threat to social order, and in June 1650 the Rump appointed a special committee to report 'on the several abominable practices of a sect called Ranters'. One writing of particular concern to the committee was Clarkson's recent *A Single Eye All Light, No Darkness*, and, it being attributed simply to 'L.C.', a search was instigated for its author. But the committee's main responsibility was to draw up a bill to put an end to Ranter activity, and in August an 'Act for the Punishment of Atheistical, Blasphemous and Execrable Opinions' was passed making it a punishable offence to deny 'the necessity of civil and moral righteousness amongst men'. Liable to arrest was any person claiming

> *him or her self, or any mere creature, to be very God, or*
> *to be infinite or Almighty, or in honour, excellence,*
> *majesty and power to be equal, and the same with the*
> *true God, or that the true God, or the Eternal Majesty*
> *dwells in the creature and no where else.*

While the wording of the Act did not exactly reflect Ranter ideas – Ranters did not claim, for example, to *be* God – it clearly aimed to outlaw their beliefs with the use of stiff penalties.

The Act also sought to outlaw, in wording which would also have embraced a good number of non-Ranters (and possibly one or two of its drafters, one would have thought), 'uncleanness, profane swearing, drunkenness, filthiness, brutishness ... stealing, cozening and defrauding others ... murder, adultery, incest, fornication, sodomy' and professing that 'heaven and happiness consisteth in the acting of these and such things' and that there is no such thing as sin 'but as a man or woman judgeth thereof'. Indeed, its intent may well have been to tighten up the law on a wide raft of issues, such as sabbath-breaking, blasphemy and sexual licence, using the appearance of Ranter writings as a pretext. But Coppe, then already in prison, was clear (we might say with good reason) that both this Act and one passed a few months earlier making adultery illegal 'were put out because of me, thereby secretly intimating that I was guilty of the breach of them', and he issued a 'Remonstrance, Vindication and Attestation' from his cell in Newgate. Judges who had the responsibility of enforcing the Act appear to have reflected the spirit in which it was passed, coming down firmly on those who publicly denied a distinction between right and wrong and ignoring others whose religious opinions, though unorthodox, appeared to be sincerely held.

The extent to which Ranters posed a real threat to good order is hard to assess. Justice Durant Hotham once told his friend George Fox that 'had not the Quakers come, the Ranters had over-run the nation', though he could have meant several things by that. On one level their aggressive outpourings and lewd behaviour could be put down to insanity, but their contemporaries clearly perceived something more was going on. The timing of the Ranters' emergence is one clue, and it may be no coincidence that Ranter tracts begin to appear as news spread of the crushing of the Levellers at Burford: indeed, Coppe bitterly alludes to the killing of the Levellers in chapter 3 of his *A Fiery Flying Roll*, written shortly after the event, and Joseph Salmon's

A Rout, A Rout, published the same year, directly addresses the behaviour of the army:

> *You are led forth in a way of vengeance upon your adversaries; you sentence and shoot to death at your pleasure; it little moves you to trample upon the blood of your enemies; this is your victory, glory and triumph.*

Was 'Ranting', then, in part a way of dealing with the disillusionment and despair that may have overtaken many whose hopes of significant political change were high at the beginning of 1649? Were the violent language and unorthodox literary style adopted by Ranters signs of a loss of faith in the value of discourse and debate, a conscious rejection of accepted modes of communication? If so, Ranterism may well have posed a perceivable threat, particularly when it began to take root among folk for whom the future looked bleak. As Christopher Hill has suggested, the idea that there is no such thing as sin might sound harmless enough in time of social peace, but it could become dangerous in a revolutionary atmosphere when some in the lower classes begin to take it literally.[7] In Frank McGregor's words, 'Ranterism articulated the ideology of a counter-culture; the society of masterless men and women: the vagrants, itinerants, cottagers, and urban immigrants.'[8] 'There was something about [Ranterism's] intransigence, its blunt nonconforming irreverence, its rough materialism and perhaps its appeal to an ancient, deep-rooted peasant communism', writes A. L. Morton, 'that made a strong appeal to many Englishmen of the lower orders.'[9] Among those who found traditional Puritan doctrines unable to lift them from guilt and despair, antinomian release from the constraints of the moral law could be attractive (as even Bunyan found). Though perhaps it was not just the Ranters' liberating theology that people found seductive: as Nigel Smith points out, their use of ritual and narcotics might also have been 'seen as a form of social escape'.[10]

One reason why Ranters looked so threatening lay in the authority they claimed in their speaking and writing: their explicit rejection of the claims of the ecclesiastical and political powers. Far from being a sign of madness, their profession to be speaking the words of God, even (or especially) in oaths, sounds like a defiant statement that God is now literally using the base things of the world to confound the mighty, that the meek really are about to inherit the earth. ('Base' is a favourite word for Coppe, perhaps linked to his understanding of the close tie between humans and animals.) Hence we have Coppe's assertions such as 'the word of the Lord came expressly to me'; his frequent use of the expression 'thus saith the Lord'; his claim that his tract *A Fiery Flying Roll* is 'A word from the Lord to all the great ones of the earth'; and his use of expressions like 'that excellent Majesty which dwells in the writer' and 'Eternal God, myself'. Coppe explicitly states in the Preface to *A Fiery Flying Roll* that 'the visions and revelations of God, and the strong hand of eternal invisible almightiness, was stretched out upon me, within me, for the space of four days and nights, without intermission'. Writing just a few months after the execution of Charles Stuart, his frequent references to the 'eternal Majesty', 'excellent Majesty' and 'divine Majesty' indwelling him would not have been lost on his readers. Swearing was also, Smith has argued, a way of manifesting that one had 'privileged knowledge':[11] for Coppe, 'there was 'swearing ignorantly, in the dark, vainly, and ... swearing in the light, gloriously'.

Ranters might appear even more threatening when they argued the social and economic equality of every person. Like Winstanley (but *un*like the Levellers themselves), Ranters were often happy to accept the title 'levellers', and Coppe spoke of God as 'that mighty Leveller', warning his readers that the Lord will come 'with a vengeance, to level ... your honour, riches' and make those 'that are greater and richer than [their] fellow-creatures, even as low as may be, and so will make all equal...'. Passages in the New Testament such as Acts 4.32 – which recounts how some of the earliest Christians held nothing privately but had all things in common (and which the Ranters extended to spouses, of course) – and the Letter of James, with its fulminations against the rich, were employed in Ranter circles: 'Thus saith the Lord', wrote Abiezer Coppe in his *A Fiery Flying Roll*, 'kings, princes, lords, great ones, must bow to the poorest peasants; rich men must stoop to poor rogues, or else they'll rue for it.' 'Howl, howl, ye nobles, howl honourable, howl ye rich men for the miseries that are coming upon you.'

God will come upon the rich like a highwayman, Coppe wrote elsewhere, saying:

> *Thou hast many bags of money, and behold now I come as a thief in the night, with my sword drawn in my hand, and like a thief as I am I say deliver your purse, deliver sirrah! deliver or I'll cut thy throat! Deliver my money to such as poor despised Maul of Dedington in Oxonshire ... deliver my money which thou hast to ... poor cripples, lazars, yea to rogues, thieves, whores, and cut-purses, who are flesh of thy flesh, and every whit as good as thy self in mine eye ... The plague of God is in your purses, barns, houses, horses, murrain will take your hogs, O (ye fat swine of the earth) who shall shortly go to the knife, and be hung up in the roof ... have ALL things common, or else the plague of God will rot and consume all that you have.*

Coppe's take on Christ's promise to come as a 'thief in the night' is not only particularly creative, it is also difficult to imagine, as Clement Hawes says, 'a more pointed challenge to the legitimacy of a certain order of property relations, and thus to the subjective divisions they produce, than this'. Coppe's reference to the concretely suffering figure of 'Maul of Dedington' 'achieves a further effect of raw immediacy'.[12] Like Quakers, Coppe scorned all social rank or status: he alludes to Mary's Magnificat as he warns that 'the day of the Lord of Hosts shall be upon every one that is proud, and lofty, and upon every one that is lifted up, and he shall be brought low', and even ignores social distinctions when he welcomes the reader of his first tract, *A Fiery Flying Roll*, shifting from 'My dear one' to 'All or none' to 'Everyone under the sun'!

৭৽৻৻

A *Fiery Flying Roll* exemplifies the unique and highly unconventional literary style of some Ranter writings: no less an authority than John Carey, Emeritus Merton Professor of English Literature at Oxford, has spoken of Coppe's work conveying its message with 'unprecedented dramatic force'.[13] While one chapter will contain dire warnings to the powerful to share their wealth with the poor, another will offer a detailed, dramatic and on one level simply comic account of the writer's own encounter with a poor beggar, and his struggle with the 'external' challenge of giving alms and the inner workings of his own mind. Superficially Coppe's writing could be dismissed as the product of insanity, both in terms of its content and style, and some of his contemporaries did indeed refer to his 'strange and fearful strain' and 'phantastick style'. But a closer reading reveals him skilfully and imaginatively employing a range of biblical images to produce a searing, if not prophetic, indictment of the injustices of his day and culpability of those who profess religion yet turn their backs on the poor.

By drawing upon his knowledge of the classics and biblical languages gained at school and university, Coppe mocks those who suppose that learning is the key to religious understanding; and even his highly unorthodox style may be a statement that, as Nicholas McDowell remarks, 'the inner Word renders the categories of knowledge ordered by grammar, syntax, translation, typography, by the written word itself – even Scripture – irrelevant'.[14] In Coppe's writing, even a seemingly insignificant episode – an exchange with a beggar – can highlight the powerful influences at work both within the individual and wider society. And when, as he frequently does, Coppe employs graphic images of violence and carnage, the result can be, as he presumably intended, both disturbing and threatening.

Yet Coppe was more about rhetoric than action: he consciously distanced himself from levelling by the sword and by digging, and forged no programme to bring about the kind of economic transformation he announced. In this he differed from the True Leveller Gerrard Winstanley, although, like Winstanley's Diggers, Ranters did believe that Christ would return, in spirit, to indwell humankind and enable all to live without possessions in community with each other and God. Indeed, the divine inspiration which they now claimed to enjoy they understood as an early manifestation of the new age, a conviction which led them to make some bold appeals to the new emerging powers to practise an ethic of peace and bring that age nearer. As Joseph Salmon writes in tract *A Rout, A Rout* (1649),

> *he that does come, will come, and will not tarry; behold he comes with recompense: you are afraid to lay down your swords, lest you should lose your liberties; but the Lord will recompense this seven-fold in your bosom, he is coming forth to make you free to suffer a blessed freedom, a glorious liberty, a sufficient recompense for the loss of all outward glories ... The Lord will honour you with meekness; you shall be the fame of the world, for true valour and spiritual courage ... when you are become children of this new birth, you shall be able to play upon the hole of the asp, and to dwell with the cockatrice in his den, oppression and tyranny shall be destroyed before you ...*

Salmon here writes as a soldier to 'my fellow soldiers', the commanders of the army.

There is also the question how far Ranters might have sought to identify with the poor and landless whose interests they appear to wish to promote in their writings. Despite his affectation to have been 'given the tongue of the learned, though he knoweth not letters' – a ploy, perhaps, to amplify his role as the mouthpiece of God – Coppe was a star pupil at Warwick School and a student at two Oxford colleges, and there is a telling sentence in one of Clarkson's tracts where he defines the 'oppressed' as the 'yeoman, farmer, the tradesman and the like'. But despite any lack of intent to pursue economic change, or basis from which any such campaign might be launched, the language and tone of many Ranter writings clearly, as they no doubt hoped, spread fear and apprehension abroad. As Frances Dow has suggested, even if Coppe and Clarkson's appeal to primitive biblical communism 'did not constitute a coherent plan for economic or political revolution by any means ... in the hands of conservatives such extravagant utterances could conveniently be used as a stick with which to beat all radicals, whatever their views.'[15]

The Blasphemy Act of 1650 did curtail some Ranting activity. All copies of Coppe's *A Fiery Flying Roll* – a book the Commons described as containing 'many horrid blasphemies, and damnable and detestable opinions, to be abhorred by all good and godly people' – were ordered to be seized and 'burnt by the hand of the hangman', and Coppe himself was examined by a parliamentary committee and sent back to Newgate. His examination seems to have been an entertaining affair, reports suggesting that the accused 'disguised himself into a madness, flinging apples and pears [another report says nutshells] about the room'! Bauthumley's *The Light and Dark Sides of God* was also condemned as blasphemous and its author bored through the tongue. One relieved observer noted that 'before the late act against the Ranters, they spake boldly; now they dare not'. Salmon was held for six months, Clarkson was (illegally) sentenced to banishment, and several dozen other Ranters and near-Ranters, including Coppin and Thomas Tany, were imprisoned. Both Bauthumley and Salmon were also cashiered from the army, along with other officers and rank and file, suggesting Ranter ideas were having some purchase there.

Once arrested, though, most Ranters were happy to recant (as, incidentally, had been Roger Brearley of Grindleton when tried in 1616), and this points to the conclusion that the purpose of the Act might have been less to punish offenders with jail than secure recantations and drive unwanted opinions and ideas from public view. In this it was not entirely successful, for Ranters hardly disappeared from the scene at this point. In fact, their tactic of recanting – to which they could hardly have had any 'principled' objection, and for which they would not have considered themselves in line for eternal punishment – might have been precisely to ensure that their ideas did not die out but simply go back underground temporarily.

တသ

Ranterism, if we can use that term, seems to have spread over a wide area. In his pioneering study in the 1970s, A. L. Morton found evidence of it in Coventry (an important centre) and other Midland towns, and in counties as far apart as Yorkshire, Norfolk, Oxfordshire, Gloucestershire, Surrey and Cornwall.[16] Yet Ranters flourished only for two or three years at most, their most active period, certainly in literary terms, being 1649–51. But if their political and social impact was, in the long term, negligible, they provide a fascinating glimpse of how a collection of disempowered, but highly imaginative and 'inspired' people, struggled with feelings of disillusionment and disappointment in the aftermath of a series of events which had once appeared so full of hope.

CHAPTER FIVE

Quakers

I F THE LEVELLERS and Diggers proved unable to change the world in the 1650s, the Quakers looked as though they just might. From very humble beginnings in 1652, they numbered 5,000 by 1654, around 20,000 by 1657 and possibly 60,000 by the end of the decade. As Hugh Barbour has written, had that pace of growth been maintained 'the world would have turned Quaker within a generation'.[1] And it was not just their numbers that made them appear a threat to good order: the perceived similarity of their ideas to those of the Levellers and especially the Ranters caused real concern among those with a vested interest in the *status quo*.

The critical figure in the origin of the movement – though he was not its only early leader – was George Fox. Born in 1624, Fox seems to have spent much of his youth despairing of finding any spiritual help from others, giving up first on the priests of the Church and then on the 'separate preachers'. There was, he noted in his journal, 'none among them all that could speak to my condition'. Then at the age of 23 he experienced an 'opening from the Lord', a direct revelation from on high; and this was given him, he later understood, not only because every human agent who might have been able to help him had been deluded by sin, but to ensure that God received all the credit for his new-found faith. Fox's 'opening' confirmed for him the importance of knowing the grace and power of God 'experimentally', by experience. Even when knowledge or understanding gained through revelation was later confirmed by a text from the Bible, the experience of the 'Word within' was always far more satisfying to the soul than any encounter with the 'Word without'.

Within 12 months Fox was embracing the possibility of living the perfect life. This came about as a consequence of another vision, one in which he first found himself sharing the experience of Adam in all his 'innocency' before the fall, and then 'taken up in spirit' beyond that 'to see into another or more steadfast state ... even into a state in Christ Jesus that should never fall'. Fox became convinced that men and women had the potential to free themselves from their 'old life', with its enslavement to sin and temptation, and experience perfection; and those who underwent this transformation or 'convincement', Fox believed, felt themselves to be separate from those who had not shared its blessings. Another Quaker leader, Edward Burrough, understood that 'the saints of God may be perfectly freed from sin in this life so as no more to commit it'.

Following a spell in jail for disrupting church services and making known his 'blasphemous' opinions, Fox began to draw together disparate groups in the north of England who shared his disillusionment with organized religion and conviction that true faith could only come direct from God. Among these were Seekers, who had links with some of the Ranters, and whose worship was characterized by long periods of silence and fasting and who stressed the importance of waiting submissively 'for the Lord to reveal himself'. Fox also spent time with groups of Baptists – many of whom he claims to have won over to his teaching – and attracted others who, perhaps having been in trouble over a refusal to pay rents or tithes, saw his emerging movement as a vehicle for political and economic change. In 1652, following a vision on Pendle Hill, Lancashire, in which he saw a 'great people to be gathered', Fox became convinced that he must form a new church, a decision that gave considerable momentum to his endeavours. Fox had already begun calling together what he called 'meetings of Friends' (anticipating the name the movement was to choose for itself) in the late 1640s, and it was the emotional outbursts and trembling which characterized these meetings – as the participants experienced the 'breaking forth of the power of God' – that gave rise to the nickname 'Quakers'.

The phenomenal growth of the Quaker movement in its early days owed much to Fox's skills as a preacher: operating in the open air, he was able to draw many hundreds at a time to hear him preaching and, like an early Billy Graham, he sought – and secured – mass responses. Yet it was not the novelty of his teaching that attracted converts: when a person was 'convinced' by Fox, as Leo Damrosch has pointed out, 'it was not a question of learning something he or she didn't already know. Every one of the distinctive Quaker beliefs or attitudes was already current.' What did inspire people was 'the realization that an actively charismatic movement might replace their former passivity and isolation'.[2]

Fox was not alone in spreading his message, and in the early days he may simply have been recognized as a co-worker in the movement rather than its leader. Much of the Quakers' early success was due to other travelling preachers such as James Parnel – known because of his youth as the 'Quaking boy' – who brought the word to Essex in 1655 and converted many across the county before his arrest and early death in jail. Fox's conversion, early in the piece, of Margaret Fell was also important, her pastoral and administrative skills contributing significantly to the early success of the movement. A member of the gentry, and wife of Judge Thomas Fell – whose support and protection of Fox and his followers was to prove invaluable – Fell allowed her home, Swarthmoor Hall, to serve as the first headquarters of the Quakers. The big Quaker outreach to the rest of England and Wales in 1654, which later extended to Ireland, across Europe and to the Americas, was organized from there.

Much influenced by his own experience, Fox placed enormous emphasis on the importance of receiving faith directly from God: the inward working of the Spirit was to be valued above the letter of Scripture. Fox was clear that the mandate he had received from God was to 'turn people to that inward light, spirit and grace ... even that divine Spirit which would lead them into all truth', and this became the core of his message. Hence Quakers stressed the 'inner light' within each person, what more conventional Puritans might have preferred to call the 'in-dwelling of the Holy Spirit', and urged people to 'look to the Light within their own consciences' and 'by the leadings of that Light ... come to God, and work out their salvation'. Anne Audland saw the mind as the 'book of conscience' upon which the Scriptures were written: experience develops as each imprint of the Word is made and the individual begins to understand the book God has given them.

The term 'the Lamb's War' – drawn from references in the Book of Revelation to Christ overcoming his enemies – was widely used by Quakers to describe the inward struggle that all must endure to overcome the old nature, with its pride and self-will. As James Nayler, a co-leader with Fox in the movement's early days, put it,

> *The Lamb's War you must know, before you can witness his kingdom ... in whomsoever [the Lamb] appears, and calls them to join with him herein ... with all their might ... that he may form a new man, a new heart, new thoughts, and a new obedience ... and there is his Kingdom.*

These beliefs shaped Quakers' attitudes to the established Church: if all men and women had the 'light within', Quakers asked, what need was there of a priest to mediate God to them or a 'learned professor' to explain them the Bible? What could such 'teachers' provide that could not be discerned or experienced directly from the Almighty? Fox himself was clear that Christ spoke to him 'without the help of any man, book or writing' (a not uncommon claim among 'radicals') and that it was 'not the letter, nor the writing of the Scripture' which saved people's souls, but the 'ingrafted Word'. Some Quakers attested that it was possible to know Christ without reading a page of Scripture, even that the Bible was 'not the word of God but only a dead letter'. Others even went so far as to publicly burn their Bibles to make the point, but if this was a rather extreme position, most would have concurred with the proposition revealed to Fox in his 'opening from the Lord', that 'to be bred at Oxford or Cambridge was not sufficient to fit a man to be a minister of Christ'. Fox had no hesitation in encouraging others to follow his practice of going into parish churches to 'challenge the divine calling' of the paid clergy, and hundreds of Quakers were arrested for just such action in the 1650s.

Quakers rejected much of the Church's teaching – or, more precisely, the way that the Church interpreted the faith. Critics accused Quakers of denying the Trinity and heaven and hell, though they themselves claimed that they *did* hold these truths, but in an internal sense. The Judgment, they argued, might be just as powerfully experienced in this life, in the individual's heart and conscience, as in the next: as the early Quaker Isaac Penington put it, 'the great judgment is already begun (this we know, who have tasted of it)'. John Bunyan was concerned that Quakers did not believe that 'the Jesus Christ who was crucified 1600 years ago' had satisfied God's demand for 'justice for the sins of the people', that human guilt could only be dealt with by the individual 'believing what another man hath done by himself without us on the cross, without the gates of Jerusalem'. But Christ's action in history, Quakers argued, was of little consequence unless people enjoyed an inward, spiritual experience of him in the present. Quakers also rejected allegations that they did not share the widespread expectation of Christ's Second Coming: they did, they argued, but understood it 'spiritually' in the sense that Christ had come to all who had experienced 'convincement'. Many believers of a more orthodox hue remained unconvinced, however, sharing with a Durham churchman a sense of despair that 'a man may be a Quaker Christian without express knowledge of Christ in the outward, either of his name, nature, laws or offices. The great Mogul hath this religion as much as George Fox. This lays aside all that Jesus was, did, taught and suffered.'

Quakers' 'internalizing' of key doctrines made them impatient of the Church's worship and sacraments. If Christ had already come, they argued, what need was there to anticipate his return in the Communion, or to have one special day a week, or seasons like Christmas and Easter, to remember him? Christ has now come to sup with those who open the door to him, Quakers said, quoting Revelation 3.20, and this 'supper' supersedes that instituted by St Paul in I Corinthians 11 in which believers are instructed to break bread 'until he comes'. Further, if Christ is ever present, why have special buildings for worship and preaching? Quakers believed everywhere to be equally holy and would meet often in the open air. Only when their homes became too small did they build 'Meeting Houses'. Quaker services contrasted greatly with those of the church, consisting essentially of the congregation silently seeking the guidance of the Spirit, who might sometimes move a worshipper to an ecstatic utterance.

Not surprisingly, Quakers were prominent in the campaign for the abolition of the tithe, producing a mass of propaganda, sponsoring numerous petitions and withholding their payment *en masse* while encouraging others to do the same. Between 1653 and 1659 at least 1,000 Quakers were brought to court for non-payment of the tithe. Richard Hubberthorne said he objected to the tithe because it restricted his enjoyment of his property, though he and other Quakers simply found the legal requirement that they pay for the upkeep of the established church, and the salaries of what they called its 'hireling priests', utterly contemptible. Fox referred to priests 'selling', 'trading' and even 'trafficking' the Scriptures – which 'were given forth freely, and [which] Christ commanded his ministers to preach freely' – and likened their behaviour, whenever a benefice became vacant upon the death of one of their number, to that of crows gathering around the carcass of a dead sheep. Edward Burrough, a leading spokesperson for the Quakers in the 1650s, spoke of tithes robbing the poor, being paid 'out of men's labours', and said that no trader could match the priests' ability to compel people to buy their wares! Of all the mid-seventeenth-century groups, Quakers were probably the most consistently anti-clerical. 'Whoever exposed the professors of Christianity more than [Quakers]?' asked the writer Francis Bugg at the end of the century.

Quakers made a point of disturbing church services. Sometimes their behaviour appeared simply irritating – as when, to ridicule the church's practice of allocating pews according to social status, they would deliberately sit in seats reserved for 'maids'; but they would also interrupt services, perhaps by denouncing the preacher as a false prophet or questioning the validity of baptizing children. Quakers would also heckle ministers in the street, and inscribe highly charged slogans on church doors such as 'Babylon's merchants' or 'children of the devil'. '[The Quakers'] religion consists chiefly in censuring others', bemoaned a Cheshire schoolmaster, 'and railing upon them, especially ministers, whom they despised and counted as dung of the earth, making it their ordinary practice to disturb them in their sermons.'

Part of the Quakers' appeal lay in the egalitarian nature of their theology: in contrast to Calvinists, whose belief in predestination they saw as privileging the 'elect' over everybody else, Quakers believed that all men and women had the potential to gain salvation, and to do so directly from God. 'God would have all men to be saved mark all men', Fox wrote, and neither education nor status was a barrier to understanding spiritual truths, all being equal in the sight of God. Predestination turned God into 'the most cruel of all beings', wrote William Penn, whereas Quakers believed that all had the potential to find Christ within them. '[God's] infinite spirit is not tied up to a few predestinarian electioners' argued George Whitehead, 'who only conceit they are elected, and moving grace only free for them.' In one sense the emphasis that Quakers placed on the spirit over and above Scripture was a way of rejecting, as uneducated men and women, the hegemony of a learned elite.

Quaker emphasis on the potential of God to indwell all people meant that the experience of women within the movement was of equal value to that of men: and women certainly found within the movement opportunities for involvement and responsibility not available to them in society at large. In some respects Quakers were typical of other movements of their day – for example, with the notable exception of Margaret Fell its leadership was entirely male;

but, of all the 'radical' movements of the mid-seventeenth century, Quakerism seemed particularly adept at recognizing and chan-nelling the gifts that a woman might have in the area of ecstatic prophecy, preaching and evangelism, and as a wife, mother, dis-penser of charity, correspondent and sick-visitor. The role of women who displayed these gifts, the 'mothers in Israel' as they were known, proved crucial to the growth of the movement, and Quaker women had an influence greater than their counterparts in other contemporary groupings.

The sheer volume of writing by Quaker women – perhaps 6 per cent of the movement's total output in the first 50 years of its exis-tence – indicates the role that they had in the promulgation of Quaker ideas. Much of this early writing took the form of prophecy, of statements 'received directly from God', a genre which gave women the 'authority' to deliver messages that would have seemed disturbing and even at times offensive to their readers. 'I am full of power by the Spirit of the Lord and of judgment, and of might, to declare unto you your transgressions and your sins', declared Jeane Bettris in her 1657 tract, *A Lamentation for the Deceived People*; and Margaret Killam and Barbara Patison had no compunction in entitling their 1656 tract *A Warning From the Lord ... to the Parish Teachers of this Nation, that have great sums of money for teaching the people*! In tracts addressed to the univer-sity cities, *Wo To Thee Town of Oxford* and *Wo To Thee Town of Cambridge*, Hester Biddle lambastes their learned inhabitants for their godlessness and, in the style of an Old Testament prophet, compares the wickedness of Cambridge to that of Sodom and calls upon the city to

> repent whilst thou hast time, lest I consume thee with fire ... therefore will I uncover thy nakedness and thy shame will I unfold ... the well-favoured harlot lodgeth in thee, the mother of witchcraft ... Oh Cambridge, thou art full of filth ... murdering and killing the just in you, and whipping and stocking them that the Lord hath sent you ... Remember you are warned in your lifetime and all left without excuse.

Plate 1 A portrait of the Leveller leader John Lilburne at his trial for treason at the London Guildhall in October 1649. He holds a copy of Sir Edward Coke's 'Institutes of the Laws of England'.

The manner of His Excellency Sir *Thomas Fairfax*, and the Officers of His Armie sitting in COVNCELL.

Plate 2   The General Council of the Army, chaired by General Thomas Fairfax, meeting in 1647.

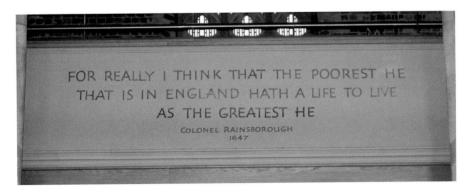

FOR REALLY I THINK THAT THE POOREST HE
THAT IS IN ENGLAND HATH A LIFE TO LIVE
AS THE GREATEST HE

COLONEL RAINSBOROUGH
1647

Plate 3   Thomas Rainsborough's famous contribution to the Putney Debates now immortalized in St Mary's Church.

The Ranters Declaration, 2

WITH

Their new Oath and Proteftation ; their ftrange Votes, and a new way to get money ; their Proclamation and Summons ; their new way of Ranting, *never before heard of* ; their dancing of the *Hay* naked, at the white *Lyon* in Peticoat-lane ; their mad Dream, and Dr. *Pockridge* his Speech, with their Trial, Examination, and Anfwers : the coming in of 3000. their Prayer and Recantation, *to be in all Cities and Market-towns read and publifhed* ; the mad-Ranters further Refolution ; their Chriftmas Carol, and blafpheming Song ; their two pretended-abominable Keyes to enter Heaven , and the worfhiping of his little-majefty, the late Bifhop of *Canterbury* : A new and further Difcovery of their black Art, with the Names of thofe that are pof- feft by the Devil, having ftrange and hideous cries heard within them, *to the great admiration of all thofe that fhall read and perufe this enfuing fubject.*

Licenfed according to order, and publifhed by M. *Stubs*, a late fellow-Ranter

Imprinted at London , by J. C. MDCL.

Plate 4   A pamphlet hostile to the Ranters, published in 1650 during their period of greatest influence.

THE QVAKERS DREAM:

OR,

The Devil's Pilgrimage in England:

BEING

An infallible Relation of their several Meetings,

Shreekings, Shakings, Quakings, Roarings, Yellings, Howlings, Trem-
blings in the Bodies, and Risings in the Bellies: With a Narrative of
their several Arguments, Tenets, Principles, and strange Doctrine: The
strange and wonderful Satanical Apparitions, and the appearing of the
Devil unto them in the likeness of a black Boar, a Dog with flaming eyes,
and a black man without a head, causing the Dogs to bark, the Swine
to cry, and the Cattel to run, to the great admiration of all that shall
read the same.

London, Printed for *G. Horton*, and are to be sold at the Royal
Exchange in Cornhil, 1655.

Plate 5   An anti-Quaker tract issued five years later. The same images have been used to
attack both movements.

Plate 6 Women were allowed to preach at Quaker gatherings, and at some Baptist meetings, but they had many detractors, even within these movements.

Iames Nailor Quaker, fot 2 howers on the Pillory at Westminster, whiped by the Hangman to the old Exchainge London, Som dayes after, Stood too howers more on the Pillory
in at the Exchainge, and there had his Tongue Bored throug with a hot Iron, &
Stigmatized in the Forehead with the Letter:B: Decem.: 17: anno Dom: 1656:

Plate 7 A depiction of the punishment meted out to Quaker leader, James Nayler, for
the crime of riding into Bristol in imitation of the original Palm Sunday.

Plate 8 An engraved portrait of
Lodowicke Muggleton from his
autobiography 'The Acts of the
Witnesses' published in 1699.

Plate 9   Jerome Willis as General Thomas Fairfax in the 1975 film *Winstanley*, based on David Caute's novel, *Comrade Jacob* and produced by Kevin Brownlow and Andrew Mollo.

Plate 10   A memorial to Gerrard Winstanley installed in 2009 in the parish church of Cobham, Surrey, where he served for a time as a churchwarden.

Plate 11 The cast of the English Civil War drama *The Devil's Whore*, produced for Channel 4 by Company Pictures and screened in 2008.

Plate 12 A demonstrator recalls Gerrard Winstanley's views on property outside the G20 world leaders summit in London in March 2009. The Digger leader was also quoted by Prime Minister Gordon Brown in a speech on the eve of the summit.

Priscilla Cotton and Mary Cole, two Quaker women imprisoned for 'prophecy' in Exeter gaol in 1655, are explicit in informing their priestly readers that, despite their knowledge of Hebrew and Greek of which they boast much, they are ignorant men. 'Silly men and women may see more into the mystery of Christ Jesus, than you', they write in their letter *To the Priests and People of England*:

> *for the apostles, that the scribes called illiterate, and Mary and Susanna (silly women [2 Timothy 3.6], as you would be ready to call them, if they were here now) these know more of the Messiah, than all the learned priests and rabbis; for it is the spirit that searcheth all things, yea, the deep things of God, you may know, and yet murder the just, and think you do God good service.*

Cotton and Cole also argue that, since 'all are one both male and female in Christ Jesus [Galatians 3.28]', the 'woman' forbidden by Paul from speaking in a church is not a literal female but the personification of 'weakness' – a trait which the *priests* show by their lack of understanding of Scripture. And hence they inform those priests that 'you yourselves are the women, that are forbidden to speak in the church, that are become women'. In Margaret Fell's estimation, Paul obviously implied that women could prophesy, since he called it improper for them to do so with their heads uncovered. Fell was clear that Paul's prohibitions on women speaking could be challenged, and cited examples from Scripture of women acting as God's messengers: 'And what is all this to women's speaking? That have the Everlasting Gospel to preach, and upon whom the promise of the Lord is fulfilled, and his Spirit poured upon them according to his Word.'

Given the speed with which the Quaker movement came together, and the disparate nature of its early membership, the writing of its women members played an important role in shaping the movement's identity. Quakers self-consciously wrote on behalf of the movement rather than as individuals, and their practice of collaborating in the writing of many of their tracts was an important statement about their sense of being a community. Quaker women might have been concerned to establish their individual 'prophetic credentials', as people to whom God spoke directly and used as channels for communicating timely messages of rebuke and warning, but they wrote primarily to highlight their connection to a wider network. As Catie Gill has observed, even personal testimonies by early Quaker women 'are regularly used to signal group membership', and it was not unusual for Quaker texts to be ascribed, not to a person or persons by name, but to 'those who are scornfully called Quakers'.[3]

Women were also important in spreading the word by preaching. We know from the testimony of Richard Hubberthorne, generally a well-informed source, that both of England's university towns first heard the Quaker message from women: Oxford through Elizabeth Fletcher and Elizabeth Leavens, and Cambridge via the testimony of Mary Fisher and Elizabeth Williams. The first Quakers in London were also women, their tactic for arousing interest in the movement being to distribute tracts written by Fox. And women were just as likely to meet with opposition and imprisonment for their witness and evangelizing as men, as in the case of Anne Audland, who was arrested in Banbury in 1655 and tried for blasphemy before being convicted of a less serious offence. Audland was reported to have preached on one occasion to '300 people in the south'. Women were also prominent in Quaker forays against the established Church, and Barry Reay has estimated that of the more than 300 Quakers arrested for disrupting church services during the years 1654 to 1659, over one-third were women.[4]

The spiritual egalitarianism which Quakers experienced in their movement was of a piece with their view that class distinctions in society were of no importance, that God really was 'the great leveller'. Some were quite outspoken in their criticism of the landed gentry, claiming that they had acquired their status and wealth by 'fraud, deceit, and oppression'. Others, echoing the fourteenth-century hedge priest John Ball, said there 'would never be a good world so long as there was a lord in England'. To underline the point that, whether people were finely or raggedly dressed, underneath they are all the same, some Quakers adopted the habit of 'going naked for a sign'; and their generally plain attire was a public demonstration of their refusal to acknowledge dress as an advertisement of social position.

'Going naked' could also be symbolic of the innocency and perfection Quakers believed it was possible to attain, though they could also adopt the practice, or put on sackcloth and ashes, as a dramatic way of calling people to repentance: the act 'could operate as a trenchant reminder to the ungodly', as Marcus Nevitt has put it, 'of the naked truth of their need for Christ, of their need to be stripped of the corrupt trappings of the world of the flesh'.[5] They might also use it for more overtly political purposes, as in the case of Elizabeth Fletcher who, 'in obedience to ye Lord', went naked through the streets of Oxford 'as a sign against that hypocritical profession they then made there, being then Presbyterians and Independents, which profession she told them the Lord would strip them of, so that their nakedness should appear'. In acting in this way, too, Quakers were no respecter of persons, and Samuel Pepys records with astonishment an incident in Westminster Hall in 1667 when, a large crowd having assembled to hear the King speak, a Quaker 'came naked through the hall, only very civilly tied about the privies to avoid scandal, and with a chafing-dish of fire and brimstone upon his head did pass through the Hall, crying, "Repent! Repent!"'

Quakers also, famously, offended against social custom by refusing to remove their hats when in the presence of their 'superiors', and by using the familiar 'thee' and 'thou' form of address with those of high rank as well as low. Fox claimed divine sanction for this practice, noting in his journal that 'when the Lord sent me forth into the world, he forbade me to put off my hat to any, high or low; and I was required to "thee" and "thou" all men and women, without any respect to rich and poor, great and small'. Some Quakers argued that they remained 'hatted' in the presence of superiors, not so much as a sign of disrespect to them, but because only God was worthy of such respect. Others, though, fuelled their critics' worst fears by speaking explicitly against social and economic distinctions: 'I find no room ... in Scripture', said the Westminster Quaker Edward Billing, 'for the whole rabble of duke, marquess, lord, knight gentleman by patents'. Quakers also refused to take the oath in court, seeing such a requirement as an insult to people who claimed to be scrupulous in maintaining their honesty, and as a breach of the Third Commandment.

Quaker contempt for social distinctions also extended to the economic inequality which underpinned them. Francis Howgill applied the teaching of Acts 4 – 'as many as were possessors of lands or houses sold them ... and distribution was made unto every man according as he had need' – to his own time; and, like Diggers, Quakers railed against those who fenced off for their own use land which had originally been given by God for all to share. 'The earth is the Lord's ... He hath given it to the sons of men in general, and not to a few lofty ones which lord it over their brethren', wrote Benjamin Nicholson in 1653. Fox himself was concerned to see land lying waste and deliberately kept from those who were hungry, and thought one remedy would be for old monastic properties and glebes to be given over to the poor. Churches, stately homes and even Whitehall, he suggested, would be more useful as almshouses.

Whether Quakers went so far as Diggers in calling for the overthrow of property as such is a moot point: one of their critics in 1655 warned that 'such as now introduce thou and thee will (if they can) expel mine and thine, dissolving all property into confusion'; and the leader of the Diggers, Gerrard Winstanley, once reportedly told Edward Burrough that he believed the Quakers 'are sent to perfect that work which fell in their hands'. A pamphlet by Richard Blome in 1659 mentioned 'some talk by some Quakers of dividing men's estates and having all things common'. However, Barry Reay argues that Quakers probably did not go as far as Diggers in espousing communism, envisaging rather 'a nation of small producers, with some limitations on the accumulation of wealth'.[6]

While Quakers felt a clear sense of calling to tackle social injustice, there is little evidence that they developed a coherent political philosophy. Fox was clear that experience of 'convincement' led of necessity to social action, and for many Quakers the 'Lamb's War' had as much an outward dimension as an inward. 'The Lamb ... hath called us to make war in righteousness for his name's sake, against hell and death, and all the powers of darkness', wrote Edward Burrough. Furthermore this 'war' would have a political edge, consistent with the Quaker position on equality: 'arise, sound forth the everlasting word of war and judgment in the ears of all nations ... wound the lofty, and tread under foot the honourable of the earth ... and the Lamb shall get the victory.' But, as Hugh Barbour points out, direct political action by Quakers, at least before 1658, in practice amounted to little more than appeals against persecution and tithes.[7] Quakers supported Parliament in its revolt against the king, and wanted an end to the Church and the introduction of laws enshrining freedom of worship, but, until the political crisis provoked by Cromwell's death, few saw the need for concerted political action.

Quakers were by no means all pacifists in the 1650s. As Christopher Hill points out, many of their leaders were ex-soldiers – including James Nayler, Richard Hubberthorne and Edward Billing – and many other Quakers served in the army or navy.[8] Fox recorded that he refused a commission in 1651 on pacifist grounds, though Hill considers his decision may have been based as much on his political objections to the government of the Commonwealth as any pacifist principle. Fox and other Quaker leaders appear to have been broadly supportive of the army through the 1650s, and some Quakers re-enlisted in 1659. Quakers were actively recruiting among the army in 1659, and at least one of their members raised a militia to counter a co-ordinated attack on them in Cheshire led by Sir George Booth. The Quakers' first official declaration of absolute pacifism in all circumstances was not made until January 1661, though to what extent this was occasioned by a change of heart or external factors is debatable.

That Quakers were so universally feared towards the end of the decade is on one level surprising, given that they lacked any real strategy for bringing about the changes they sought; and in his detailed study of Quaker involvement in the traumatic events of 1659–60 Barry Reay concludes that hostility towards them owed as much to perception as to reality.[9] Yet Quakers gave every reason to be feared. Their refusal to show proper respect to their betters, for example, could have far-reaching implications in a culture deeply informed by notions of hierarchy and status: since 'the whole world is governed by superiority and distance in relations', said one of their critics, 'when that's taken away, unavoidably anarchy is ushered in'. Military leaders such as Henry Cromwell and General George Monck considered the Quakers' attitude towards their superiors incompatible with army discipline, and Monck once wrote to Oliver Cromwell to warn him against allowing more Quakers to be recruited to the army.

Further, the Quakers' chief political demands by 1659 – liberty of conscience, and the abolition of tithes, the universities and the State church – amounted to essentially a call for the overthrow of the whole clerical establishment, and those who understood how official religion functioned to hold society together, and keep each person in their place, saw only too well the potential consequences of the Quakers' position. Fox denied that Quakers were against magistracy or wanted to reignite civil conflict in the 1650s, but not all were persuaded. 'The Quakers are not only numerous but dangerous', said one of their opponents in 1656, 'and the sooner we put a stop, the more glory we shall do to God, and safety to this commonwealth …'.

Quakers also aroused hostility among people who had less of a stake in the established order, who may have been as much 'in contempt of government' as Quakers themselves were often accused of being. Quakers liked to believe that any mobs who attacked them were provoked into action by the authorities, and in some cases this was true, but, as David Underdown has pointed out, Quakers were often seen as a threat to the 'familiar, customary order to which many of the lower orders were as firmly attached as their social superiors: undermining the authority of husbands over wives and children, challenging the comfortably familiar even if inequitable local hierarchy, splitting parish communities'.[10]

‌

Quakers

Some two thousand Quakers were gaoled for refusing to pay tithes, speaking in church and other offences, and while some sentences were light there is evidence that, in the seventeenth century as a whole, more than 400 Quakers died as a result of harassment or imprisonment. Women were treated no less brutally than men, as the distressing cases of Margaret Newby, who was kept in the stocks in November for 17 hours and died as a consequence, and Margaret Killam, who was tied to a horse with her arms bound, testify. There may be no hyperbole in Richard Baxter's assertion that Quakers in his day 'were dragged away daily to the common gaol … so that Newgate was filled with them. Abundance of them died in prison, and yet they continued their assemblies still.'

Quakers were associated with witchcraft, sexual immorality and even papist subversion, and the term 'Quaker' was often used, like 'Anabaptist' and 'Ranter', as a catch-all term of abuse. Many critics genuinely could not tell any difference between Friends and Ranters, and in fact thought Quakers worse than Ranters because they held the same opinions but gave them an outward religious gloss. Both movements, the Baptist Thomas Collier wrote in 1657, have 'no Christ but within; no Scripture to be a rule; no ordinances, no law but their lusts, no heaven nor glory but here, no sin but in the consciences of ignorant ones': the only difference is that Quakers 'smooth it over with an outward austere carriage before men, but within are full of filthiness'.

John Bunyan also thought that Quaker ideas were the same as those held by the Ranters except that 'the Ranters had made them threadbare at an ale-house', and Richard Baxter thought Quakers 'were but the Ranters turned from horrid profaneness and blasphemy, to a life of extreme austerity on the other side. Their Doctrines were mostly the same with the Ranters.' Lodowicke Muggleton linked Quakers with 'atheistical Ranters' and constantly denounced and damned them. As Nigel Smith has commented, 'the fierce enthusiasm and violent language of the early Quakers led many to fear them as a socially subversive phenomenon'.[11]

A group that split off from the movement in 1654, the 'Proud Quakers', certainly did display Ranterish tendencies, using profane language, behaving wildly and rejecting any form of organized worship. Fox consistently opposed them, though Nayler shared some of their views. Nayler's claim to spiritual perfection also echoed Ranter expressions. By 1656 Fox was keen to highlight differences between Quakers and Ranters, noting in his journal how the latter grew 'light and loose' at their meetings on account of the tobacco and ale they consumed, and that they 'sung, whistled and danced', particularly if a Quaker was preaching: they were part of the enemy in the Lamb's War. Other Quaker leaders denounced Nayler's supporters as Ranters and began warning Quakers to beware of the Ranter spirit. When Margaret Fell was advised that some Ranters in the south were claiming there to be no difference between themselves and Quakers, save that the latter 'did not see all things to be theirs', she firmly rejected the idea and reproved Ranters' immoral behaviour, affirming that Friends denied all Ranters and their principles.

Quakers were also linked with Anabaptists, still a code word for the threat of revolution and anarchy. Newsbooks like *Mercurius Politicus* and *The Publick Intelligencer* could report that 'Anabaptists and Quakers were joined together to cut the throats of all the ministers and magistrates' in the West Country, and that in Norfolk a gentleman had found it politic to keep an arsenal of weapons in his house 'to secure himself against Quakers and Anabaptists who he feared would rise to cut his throat'. Prince Charles was assured by a correspondent of the readiness of his future subjects 'to defend ourselves against the storm of Quakers and Anabaptists', and once Charles was on the throne a Bristol gentleman reflected how the Protestant religion had 'been in great danger of being rooted out by Anabaptists, Quakers, and atheists'. The events at Münster were of course also evoked, one book circulating in 1659 rejoicing in the title *The English Quakers the German Enthusiasts Revived*. Another writer, noting the Quakers' practice of meeting at night, thought 'these unseasonable dark assemblies of theirs [to be] much like the night-meetings of the Anabaptists of Münster, which afterwards proved fatal to that city'.

At its height, opposition towards the Quakers was intense. Perhaps unsurprisingly, much of it came from the gentry and clergy, who felt particularly threatened. One minister considered that he had a Christian duty to stone Quakers, and claimed that if St Paul were still alive he would agree. A Bath clergyman said he wanted 'three or four Quakers hanged for an example', and another, in Lancashire, told a Quaker that the local magistrates were at fault 'in that they did not sheath their swords in the bowels of such blasphemers as you are'. When aired in the pulpit such views could have a powerful effect on ordinary folk, and the growth of opposition to Quakers across all sections of society may have had much to do with the attitude of clergy.

Actual violence against Quakers was not unknown, with attacks on individual men and women and theft from their property. In Sussex, Margery Caustock and her daughter were punched and stoned for attending a Quaker meeting, and, in Wales, Elizabeth Holme was chained to the wall of a prison cell and forced to drink by sucking on a straw through a hole in the door. When Elizabeth Fletcher and Elizabeth Leavens reached Oxford with the Quaker message they were doused in muddy water, tortured with water from a pump, beaten and then whipped. Attempts to break up Quaker meetings could sometimes be comical – as when an opponent threw a dead cat and other creatures into an open-air gathering and then let loose his hounds – but others were more serious. In a number of towns the officials closed down Quaker gatherings, in others attacks by mobs were reported. With Quaker leaders able to draw thousands to an open-air meeting, they would undoubtedly have appeared to local communities a threatening presence.

If some reactions to Quakerism were patently over the top, the behaviour of one of their early leaders, James Nayler, hardly helped to reduce public anxiety. In a celebrated incident in October 1656, Nayler, who until this point may have been more influential among the Quakers than Fox, rode into Bristol on a donkey to the accompaniment of adoring women strewing palms and crying 'holy, holy, holy'. Nayler was clearly in a tired and emotional state at the time, having travelled from London via Launceston (where Fox was in prison) and been imprisoned in Exeter, where he fasted, but he allowed himself to be led into the city in an obvious re-enactment of Christ's entry into Jerusalem on Palm Sunday. The whole episode may have been no more than a Quaker sign that Christ can enter men and women and enable them to achieve Christ's perfection and perform Christ's works, and Nayler was hardly the first (or last) to display Messianic pretensions; but it brought to the surface all the fears of the authorities about the influence and subversive potential of the movement.

Recognizing Nayler's importance and status within the movement – 'cut off this fellow and you will destroy the sect' one parliamentarian said when his case was discussed – and the opportunity that his arrest provided to weaken the Quaker cause, MPs spent six weeks denouncing him in the most hysterical manner, some even calling for him to be put to death by stoning. In the end Nayler did escape the ultimate penalty, but was subjected to almost literally a fate worse than death involving branding on the forehead with the letter 'B' for Blasphemer, the boring of his tongue, being whipped through two cities, pillorying and indefinite confinement – a trauma from which, not surprisingly, he never recovered.

Whatever else can be said about it, Nayler's action had been badly timed, providing Parliament with just the excuse it needed at that moment to curb the freedoms enjoyed by increasingly troublesome dissident minorities. Following the Nayler episode a new 'Confession of Faith' was agreed by Cromwell and Parliament, much more conservative in tone than that originally established by the Protectorate, which no one was permitted, 'by opprobrious words or writing maliciously or contemptuously to revile or reproach'. Legislation was also passed extending the powers of justices to act against all 'idle, loose and dissolute person and persons' found journeying outside their home area without 'good and sufficient cause or business', and stiff fines were set for disrupting services and not attending church or another 'meeting-place of Christians' – the definition of the latter excluding Quaker meeting houses. If these measures were not explicitly directed against the Quakers, they were not infrequently used to harass them, including those travelling in pursuit of their lawful trade. The Bristol affair also caused ructions within the Quaker community, and led some (including Fox, whose relationship with Nayler had been tense anyway) to disown him. Others, though, continued to treat Nayler as almost divine: 'thy name is no more to be called James but Jesus', wrote one of his admirers, while another claimed that she had been dead for two days until Nayler brought her back to life.

Quakers, then, made a huge impact on society in the 1650s. Their rapid numerical growth, their socially subversive behaviour and their concerted opposition to the church and the tithe made them a source of fear for many. And if their political platform for most of their first decade was modest, in 1659 they certainly stepped up a gear and wanted a piece of the action. But despite drawing into their ranks key figures from other radical movements – such as John Lilburne and Gerrard Winstanley – they were not the 'reincarnation' of these movements that many of their opponents tried to suggest (and some disillusioned radicals hoped) they were. To reiterate Barry Reay's point, in 1659 'myth swamped reality', and '[w]hat became important was not what was happening but what people thought was happening'.[12]

Reay also makes the interesting point that the Quakers unwittingly helped to precipitate the return of the Stuarts: such was the fear and anxiety that they and other sectaries provoked in the highly charged period following the death of Cromwell that people were led 'to look to the monarchy as the only salvation from social and religious anarchy'. After the Nayler incident the tide turned against Quakers, and their increasingly energetic pursuit of their aims served only to strengthen the hand of the forces of conservatism to the point where monarchy was re-established in 1660. More than anything, the Restoration was a reaction to the 'immense and boundless liberty' of the preceding year: there had simply become more freedom than most people could bear, and only the return of monarchy could save the nation.[13]

'Social and religious anarchy': the two were inextricably linked in the minds of all right-thinking people. By threatening the power and influence of the church, Quakers tore at the whole fabric of society. It was the duty of the church and its priests to instil in ordinary folk respect for their betters and obedience to the law: 'if there were not a minister in every parish', as a writer in 1660 put it, 'you would quickly find cause to increase the number of constables'. Charles' accession was therefore, to some, nothing less than an act of divine intervention, and Richard Baxter was not the only one publicly to give thanks to God for rescuing religion from subversion at the hands of the sects by a 'wonderful whirlwind'. 'God is blasting our fanatic enemies; and we are well on the way to religious as well as civil settlement' wrote a Presbyterian divine in a tract with the none-too-subtle title, *England's Grounds of Joy*.

After 1660, Quakerism lost its cutting edge, and survival rather than agitation became its chief concern. Shaken by reaction to the Nayler episode, disillusioned by the outcome of the events of 1659, and fearful what a restored monarchy would mean for them, Quakers drifted into political quietism. Perhaps as a way of distancing themselves from the violent Fifth Monarchist insurrection in 1661 – following which some Quakers were arrested – they officially declared themselves to be pacifist. Concerned also to distance his movement from the Ranters, Fox encouraged his preachers to stress human perfectability less and human sinfulness more, and he set about imposing more discipline and order on the movement at the expense of members' liberty to follow the promptings of the Spirit. This was necessary, too, with splits and factions occurring, and the movement began to adopt hierarchical structures and resemble, in the 1660s, more a denomination than a sect.

While Quaker habits such as refusing hat honour and wearing simple dress remained, activities at the more eccentric end, such as going naked for a sign and performing 'miracles', were quietly dropped as, in Christopher Hill's words, 'the inner light adapted itself to the standards of the commercial world where yea and nay helped one to prosper'. But as Hill goes on to say, 'it is as pointless to condemn this as a sell-out as to praise its realism: it was simply the consequence of the organized survival of a group which had failed to turn the world upside down'.[14] As long as the future seemed open, as it did at times in the 1650s, Quakers could remain flexible in their political and spiritual outlook: but as hopes that the kingdom of God might soon be ushered in began to fade, so some accommodation to the world as it actually turned out had to be negotiated. The Quaker historian H. Larry Ingle has argued that Fox's most enduring contribution to the development of Quakerism was not the 'inner light' but the way he circumscribed the movement's early radical individualism by developing an institutional structure to provide the discipline and unity needed for survival in Restoration England.[15] That Quakers are still flourishing 350 years later suggests that he gave it something even more lasting than that.

CHAPTER SIX

Fifth Monarchists

NONE OF THE movements which emerged in the mid-seventeenth century looked more eagerly for the second coming of Christ than the Fifth Monarchists. Many people in the 1640s and 50s understood the traumatic events that they were witnessing as signs that the last days were upon them, and some, like the Diggers, saw their action in terms of Christ 'rising up in his sons and daughters'; but only the Fifth Monarchists made a belief in Christ's return to earth to establish his rule their *raison d'être*. For them, the execution of Charles and its aftermath were unmistakeable signs that the events foretold in the Bible's prophetic books were coming to pass: these included the demise (foreseen in Daniel chapter 2) of the four great empires of the world and establishment by God of a fifth kingdom to 'stand forever'; and the reference in Revelation chapter 20 to Christ reigning with his saints on earth for a thousand years.

Belief in a 'millennium', or thousand-year reign of Christ, had been popular among the earliest Christian communities: the idea of a new order being established on earth was rooted in the soil of Jewish messianism, and further encouragement to early Christians to take it seriously was provided by sayings of Jesus such as 'the meek ... shall inherit the earth' (Matthew 5.5) and references in Paul to the whole creation waiting with eager longing for the birth of a new age (Romans 8). Yet its essentially subversive character drove it underground in the wake of the church's alliance with empire in the fourth century and its declaration as a heresy by the Council of Ephesus in 451, to the extent that it was kept alive in subsequent centuries mainly by groups and individuals on the margins of the church.

Originally, as Norman Cohn points out in his seminal work on the subject, the term 'millennium' was understood, on the basis of Revelation 20.4–6, as a kingdom of literally 1,000 years, lasting from the second coming of Christ until the final judgment: it would be ruled over, as the text of St John's revelation makes clear, by Christ and the 'martyrs for the faith' who had been raised back to life in advance of the general resurrection. However, since they expected the second coming in their own lifetime, the early Christian communities broadened their understanding of 'the martyred' to include themselves, the 'suffering faithful', and further refinements were made in view of the millennium's delayed arrival.[1] Despite popular (mis)perceptions of the term, millenarians are concerned primarily with the here and now rather than the future, with discerning the significance of the present 'propitious moment' as an opportunity to act to transform the world rather than expectations of another world in different time and space.

As old familiar landmarks began to disappear in the 1640s, many English people found a new impulse to scour the Bible and astrological works for clues of when the second coming might occur. Decoding the vision of the four-layered beast in Daniel, representing the great kingdoms of history, had occupied the minds of many theologians and seers over the centuries, and by the late Middle Ages a consensus had emerged that the empires in question were Assyria, Babylon, Greece and Rome. No indication was given in Daniel as to when the fourth kingdom would be overthrown and the fifth set up, though cryptic references to a period consisting of 'time, times and half a time' (which the Digger leader Gerrard Winstanley drew upon and which were generally taken to mean three and a half years or 1,260 days), and to other blocks of time such as 1,290 days and 1,335 days, provided suggestive clues.

Significantly, given that 'Rome' was taken to include the Holy Roman Empire, which historically had a close association with the papacy, the execution in 1649 of a king associated by many with 'popery' lifted popular expectations of an imminent arrival of the fifth monarchy, under 'king Jesus', to new heights. Extra spice was added to the mix by popular theories concerning the downfall of the Antichrist (generally understood by Puritans to be the Pope), which suggested that this could be expected in the 1650s, or 1,260 years after his rise to power at the end of the fourth century. A further twist to Daniel's prophecy was that the fourth empire, also depicted as a beast, had ten horns, plus a further smaller one which appeared when three of the original horns were plucked up by their roots. This 'little horn' spoke clearly, to some, of Charles or the Stuart dynasty in general. And Daniel also spoke of a time when the saints would take possession of the kingdom.

ৎ৽৹৵

The Fifth Monarchy movement actually arose once the feverish expectations of January 1649 had died down and 'saints' of a radical mind began to suspect that the advancement of Christ's cause, the new millennium, was being thwarted by parliament (the remnant of the Long Parliament known as the Rump) and, subsequently, Cromwell himself. Whether they approved of the execution of the king or not, many millenarians expected, in the wake of that event, rapid changes in line with their understanding of what the coming of the 'kingdom of Christ' might entail; these included, as a petition from some Norfolk millenarians to Parliament in March 1649 explained, the removal of 'the scandalous and ignorant clergy', especially from places where there are 'godly pastors'; proper observance of the Lord's Day; an end to lawyers growing rich 'by and of the ruins of poor men' and 'lords of manors [exacting] fines according to their own wills upon poor tenants'; and an end to other impositions, such as taxes, which leave 'free born English still made slaves by the marks of the Conqueror'. Had the Rump Parliament, or for that matter the army, showed a concern to make these reforms, most millenarians might well have been content; it was when it became apparent that God's work was not going to be furthered by either institution that plots to advance it from below began to be hatched.

The formal emergence of the movement can be dated to 1651 when 'divers officers and members of several congregations' met with Cromwell in London to urge him to 'press forward in promoting that glorious cause' and 'quicken the Parliament to do some honest and honourable works'. Two such meetings took place, but after the second the 'officers and members' concluded that Oliver was unsympathetic to their plea and decided to meet on their own 'to pray for a new Representative, and to preach somewhat against the old'. The main venues for these conversations were Allhallows the Great in Thames Street and St Anne's, Blackfriars, churches where some of the leading discussants – Christopher Feake, John Simpson and Henry Jessey – were based. The group included other preachers and army figures such as Hanserd Knollys, William Greenhill, Thomas Brooks, Major General Thomas Harrison, Major William Packer and Captain John Spencer; and Feake recorded that, within half an hour of their first meeting together, the group had agreed six objectives or 'General Heads of Prayer', including a commitment to see 'utterly pulled down, or brought to nothing ... whatsoever stood in the way' of Christ's kingdom. They were clear that the current parliament, the Rump, and all other institutions not in the hands of the saints, were 'pieces of the fourth monarchy', and called for a government composed of men elected because of their godliness and not on account of 'all other qualifications, of birth, riches or parts'.

The Fifth Monarchists' opposition to the Rump – shared also by many leading figures in the army – intensified in the early months of 1653. Preachers at their meetings in the spring denounced 'that accursed parliament at Westminster' and predicted that it would 'see a greater destruction ... than ever befell the Cavaliers', and then targeted Cromwell himself. There must be 'both a new Parliament and a General before the work be done', Fifth Monarchist preachers were reported as saying: 'these are not the people that are appointed for perfecting of that great work of God, which they have begun'. Before April was out Cromwell himself, for his own reasons, had lost patience with the Rump and, with military back-up, dissolved it by force.

At this point Cromwell was back in favour again with 'the pulpit men of Blackfriars', as some leading Fifth Monarchists were known, many hailing him as a 'second Moses' who had been raised up to lead his people out from bondage. Messages flowed in from all corners congratulating the army and its general on their action and expressing a conviction that the work they were now about was 'the setting up of the Kingdom of Jesus Christ'. Yet on the question of what should succeed the Rump, Fifth Monarchists displayed less unanimity: some, like the Independent minister John Rogers, argued that God had chosen Cromwell to select personally a new assembly; others considered that the army (by which they meant only its officers) or the gathered churches should vote one in; and the Baptist and former army officer John Spittlehouse thought that Cromwell should have absolute power as God's lieutenant on earth. Rogers and others stretched the symbolism of Cromwell as the 'new Moses' to the extent of calling for the new government to be modelled on the Sanhedrin which God commanded the Hebrew leader to assemble during the exodus from Egypt. Others, such as Major General Harrison, also saw the reconstitution of such an assembly as a precondition for Christ's arrival.

In the end Cromwell decided on an assembly – known generally as the Barebones Parliament after one of its members, Praise-God Barbone – whose members he and his officers chose themselves. In making their selection Cromwell's men embraced the suggestion that the assembly be drawn from 'the various forms of godliness in this nation', but while some Fifth Monarchists welcomed their action as 'such a mercy as goes beyond what we would have believed that our eyes should ever have seen', others were not so pleased. In a sermon in May, Christopher Feake affirmed that Oliver 'was not the man, that the Lord had chosen, to sit at the helm', and other preachers declared, 'by revelation', that the nation needed to return to monarchy, but from 'a new line'. The disparity of views among Fifth Monarchists and their sympathizers may have been rooted in part in conflicting expectations regarding when Christ might return and the form that his 'reign' would take. Feake's reference to the desirability of monarchy from 'a new line' suggests an anticipation of Christ appearing soon to reign 'in person', while a priority for those expecting Christ to appear less imminently would be the need for godly government during the waiting period.

Bernard Capp, who has written the best major study of the Fifth Monarchy movement, suggests that the Barebones Parliament 'was the nearest millenarianism came to capturing the [English] revolution and in many ways the high water mark of radicalism'.[2] Although only 12 of the 140 members appointed by Cromwell were recognizably Fifth Monarchists (among them Major General Harrison, John Carew and Colonel Henry Danvers), many others shared their position; in addition, two of their number were appointed to the executive body, the Council of State, and others sat on all the major committees. Cromwell's own position appeared to be sympathetic to Fifth Monarchy concerns, his speech to the new assembly in July noting that 'this may be the door to usher in the things that God has promised, which have been prophesied of' and pointing specifically to 'that prophecy in Daniel' which it was the assembly's duty 'not vainly to look at' but 'to endeavour this way'. His attribution of the events of recent years to 'the strange windings and turnings of Providence' and references to 'that series of providences wherein the Lord hitherto hath dispensed wonderful things to these nations, from the beginning of our troubles to this very day', would have resonated deeply with his Fifth Monarchist hearers, as would his call to the assembly to lead the people from the things of the flesh to the things of the spirit, and description of the moment as 'a day of the power of Jesus Christ'.

Whether this speech suggests, as John Morrill argues, that Cromwell saw the Barebones assembly as 'a this-worldly fulfilment of the promise of God to be with his people as he had been with Israel in the days of obedience' rather than 'evidence that [he] thought that the end of the world was nigh',[3] the first declaration of the assembly struck a decidedly millenarian tone, affirming their expectation of Christ's 'glorious coming ... to conquer, till he hath subdued all his enemies'. It might also have occurred to some observers that the size of the assembly was not without apocalyptic import, having exactly double the 70 members of the original Sanhedrin. (In fact, given that the assembly voted to co-opt an extra four members, it might have been understood as having even more significance, chapter 7 of the Book of Revelation noting the special place in heaven afforded the '144,000', 'sealed out of every tribe of the people of Israel'.) In the heady first weeks of the Barebones Parliament a feeling that the reign of the saints was being inaugurated spread far and wide: the Leveller leader John Lilburne thought it worth contacting Feake from his cell in Newgate to request his help, and even Feake himself wrote a hymn for his congregation expressing thanks for these 'days of joy [when] we rejoice to see proud Babylon down fall'.

Yet the Fifth Monarchists' hopes were short-lived. They lost a succession of votes in the House which would have effectively brought an end to the national church by abolishing tithes and allowing no restrictions on public preaching, and failed to secure any radical changes to the law, which they saw as another pre-requisite for the establishment of the millennium. Within just two months the Fifth Monarchist members of the assembly had lost interest in its affairs, and by late summer they had called a meeting to discuss whether they should leave the House and remonstrate against its members as 'hinderers of Reformation and not fit to govern the nation any longer'.

Cromwell himself was vilified by Fifth Monarchists. His attempts to negotiate an end to the war with the Dutch – a conflict which many saw as a way of advancing the millennium and bringing economic benefits – outraged leaders of the movement such as Feake, but the final straw was his acceptance of a resolution, which their opponents pushed through the House in their absence (at a prayer meeting) on 12 December 1653, to dissolve the (still new) assembly. The grounds given by these 'moderates' for their action was the danger the Fifth Monarchists posed to the stability of the nation by their continued (and, as they perceived it, increasingly effective) attempts to secure wholesale ecclesiastical and legal reform; but to the movement itself, the fall of Barebones did nothing less than abort the gradual progress of the millennium, and Cromwell's acquiescence of it (albeit that he claimed to have no foreknowledge of it) earned him their lasting disapprobation. To make matters worse, three days later the Army Council issued what was effectively England's first written constitution and created the position of Lord Protector, to which Cromwell was duly appointed.

Prior to Barebones' dissolution Feake had denounced Cromwell as 'the man of sin, the old dragon, and many other scripture ill names', and he and Vavasor Powell, another radical Fifth Monarchist leader, now charged the new Lord Protector with being 'the dissemblingest perjured villain in the world'. Powell offered up a public prayer, 'Lord, wilt Thou have Oliver Cromwell or Jesus Christ to reign over us', while Feake challenged his hearers to re-think their assumption that Charles had been the 'little horn' in the Danielic vision. John Rogers wanted 'no lord protector but our Lord Jesus' and denounced the new regime in vivid terms: 'Fah, fah, it stinks of the brimstone of Sodom, and the smoke of the bottomless pit'. Some Fifth Monarchists now began to assert their right to take up arms against the Protector, though their general line was that, while they had a duty to denounce the tyrant and predict his downfall, they needed a clear sign from God before using physical force.

Not surprisingly, the increasingly combative attitude of some of the Fifth Monarchist leadership provoked a reaction from Cromwell, and Feake, Powell, Rogers and Simpson – who had predicted the Protector's downfall within six months – were all arrested. Cromwell also counter-attacked by instigating a day of fasting, during which people were to repent for caring more about 'having rule in the world, than over their own hearts'. Leading Independent and General and Particular Baptist ministers also made public their disquiet about the movement's stance, noting the 'shame and contempt' that they had brought to the nation and the dishonour their action had brought to the gospel. But the movement refused to cow, and while Feake and Simpson continued to encourage the faithful from their prison at Windsor, and Rogers from his cell at Lambeth Palace, others mounted a concerted propaganda campaign to weaken the army's support for the government. Given that Cromwell's regime needed the support of the military to survive, this tactic had potentially far-reaching consequences, and Cromwell's frequent purges of the army showed how seriously he viewed the Fifth Monarchist threat.

ৼৡ

One powerful weapon in the Fifth Monarchists' armoury was the claim made by some of their members to be able to receive messages from God through dreams and visions. Like most of their radical contemporaries they held that a true understanding of God's dealings with humanity came directly through mystical experiences rather than book-learning and study at university, and their leadership were well-acquainted with the works of mystical writers such as Paracelsus and Boehme, and subject themselves to mystical experiences. The leading Welsh Fifth Monarchist Morgan Llwyd translated some of Boehme's writings into his native tongue, and his fellow countryman Vavasor Powell was described as 'a great observer of dreams, and what God might speak to himself or others by them'. As the future Fifth Monarchist Mary Cary observed in her 1648 writing *The resurrection of the witnesses*, 'every saint in a sense, may be said to be a prophet, for they are prophets to whom God discovers his secrets: and there is no true saints, but the secrets of God are discovered to them'; and when the Lord has revealed himself to the soul 'and discovered his secrets to it ... the soul cannot choose but declare them to others ... yet he that speaketh to edification, exhortation and consolation, though much with weakness, doth as truly prophesy as he that hath greatest abilities'.

The movement's most powerful visionary was Anna Trapnel, who first came to prominence when she attended the examination of Vavasor Powell at Whitehall in January 1654, just weeks after the dissolution of the Barebones assembly. During Powell's hearing Trapnel was 'seized upon by the Lord' and lay 'eleven days and twelve nights in a trance, without taking any sustenance, except a cup of small beer once in 24 hours, during which time she uttered many things ... relating to the governors, churches, ministry, universities and all the three nations'. While these utterances accentuate her own suffering and the mocking she received from others, which she compared to the experience of biblical women such as her namesake, Hannah, they also express her passionate hopes for a fifth monarchy and sense that she was living in 'overturning, overturning, overturning days':

> *Oh King Jesus thou art longed for*
> *Oh take thy power and reign*
> *And let they children see thy face.*

Describing herself as a 'poor hand maid' – the term recalled the prophecy in Joel (reiterated in Acts) that in the last times God will pour out his spirit upon his servants and handmaids – Trapnel made veiled, and sometimes not so veiled, references to Cromwell's impending downfall. The Lord, she prophesied, would 'batter' the 'great powers' – including the Protector and his army officers – and in doggerel verse told her amanuensis to

> *Write how that Protectors shall go*
> *And into graves there lie:*
> *Let pens make known what is said, that*
> *They shall expire and die.*

One report noted that Anna prayed 'for the Lord Protector that God would keep him close to himself, as he hath hitherto, so still to have his heart set upon the things of the Lord, not to be vain, nor regard earthly pomp and pleasure, and things below'. But she could also be more direct, echoing other Fifth Monarchists who had come to believe at that time that, far from being 'Gideon, going before Israel, blowing the trumpet of courage and valour', Cromwell was now a bull, running 'at many precious saints that stood in the way of him, that looked boldly in his face; he gave them many pushes, scratching them with his horn'.

Not all Trapnel's male associates welcomed her interventions – Jessey and Simpson, for example, suggested that there was more self-will than divine-will behind her fast – but the seriousness with which her utterances were received (numerous influential people visited her during her 'seizure') suggests that her influence was strong within a movement which, in general, paid enormous respect to women who appeared to be endowed with divine grace. 'Particular souls shall not only have benefit by her', said one report, 'but the universality of saints shall have discoveries of God through her'. Cromwell himself – who was warned by his informer, Marchamont

Nedham, that Trapnel 'doth a world of mischief in London, and I believe will abroad in the counties' and that there were plans to publish her prophecies which are 'insufferably desperate against your highness' person, family, relations, friends, and the government' – was not unmoved by her utterances, and on 19 January, the last day of her prophesying, the Council of State made it a treasonable offence 'to compass or imagine the death of the Lord Protector' or cast doubt on the legitimacy of his government. Trapnel was eventually arrested in Cornwall, where her prophesying also drew much attention, and imprisoned during June and July.

When a new parliament was summoned in September 1654 (a council of state having governed in the interim), Fifth Monarchists saw fresh opportunity for attack, circulating a petition calling upon the House to remove the present tyrannical regime – described as worse than that of Charles Stuart – and bring back a 'state of perfect liberty'. But the movement was by now in decline. Rumours circulated that the Fifth Monarchists were building alliances with other disaffected groups, including Baptists, former Levellers and Royalists, with a view to staging an attack on Cromwell, but the authorities acted swiftly and the threats failed to materialize. In December 1655 Powell drafted a petition entitled *A Word for God*, accusing the government of having betrayed the cause of Christ and encouraging all who felt the same way to join forces against it; and while this circulated widely and suggested that the movement still had the potential to provoke unrest, strategic arrests and counter-propaganda enabled the government to keep the lid on trouble. The year 1656 revived some millenarians' hopes that the reign of Christ was still in view – calculations suggested that 1,656 years had elapsed between the Creation and the Flood and so comparable remarkable events were anticipated – but generally, as Capp has put it, by the following year, 'the removal of the [movement's] ablest leaders and the failure of the saints' expectations sapped enthusiasm'.[4]

Despite getting weaker, however, the movement refused completely to die. The funeral of the prominent Fifth Monarchist John

Pendarves, in Abingdon in September 1656, turned into a large rally, and when those present turned to debate 'whether God's people must be a bloody people (in the active sense)' the motion was enthusiastically endorsed. The following year saw Thomas Venner, leader of a militant congregation meeting in Swan Alley, Coleman Street, attempt an uprising with some 80 followers, but this was quelled by government troops before it could begin and Venner was confined to the Tower. Rumours that Cromwell was to be made king that year aroused fierce opposition from Fifth Monarchists, not least Feake and Trapnel, and the realization in June that the Protectorate had had three and a half years in power – the 42 months (or 1,260 days) of the Beast's dominion according to Revelation – emboldened Rogers and others to declare that they would not rest until 'they had the tyrant's head from his shoulders'. Cromwell's eventual death in 1658 gave the movement one last opportunity for power, not least when his son Richard was swept aside, the Rump was restored, and Fifth Monarchists assumed key positions of authority within it, but once again their hopes for wholesale legislative reform were dashed. Hugely divided, distrusted by many of their fellow citizens and with most of their leaders under arrest, the movement witnessed the restoration of the monarchy in the person of Charles II in May 1660.

Bernard Capp describes the Fifth Monarchists as 'a pressure group rather than a new denomination or party',[5] and perhaps because they constantly anticipated the imminent reign of Jesus they never created any lasting, national organization. They did have 'representatives' and agents in many parts of the country, and there were groups of Fifth Monarchists in places as far apart as Liverpool, Oxford, Hull, East Anglia, the West Country and of course London, but they lacked any chain of command or central co-ordination. Although they had a clear identity, and regularly held their own meetings and services, in some places (notably London) Fifth Monarchist groups existed more as a 'tendency' within Baptist or

Congregational churches. The movement did not require adherence to any rigid statement of faith on the part of its members, allowing for a wide variety of opinions on matters of doctrine and practice. Indeed, such were the disagreements between the saints on issues such as baptism and salvation that John Rogers once told Cromwell that the only thing that united Fifth Monarchists in love one to another was opposition to him!

Fifth Monarchists never united on a manifesto or agreed programme, though they did share a core of ideas. Like most of their 'radical' contemporaries they opposed the Church and its tithe-funded priests, and Fifth Monarchists who served in the Barebones Parliament made abolition of tithes one of their chief concerns. The right to engage in violence was a common theme in Fifth Monarchist sermons and writings, and while this assertion distinguished them from millenarians in general, in practice it amounted to little more than a threat, since they were generally reluctant to act without a clear sign from God. When a violent insurrection *was* actually planned, such as that by Thomas Venner in London in 1657, clear differences emerged in the leadership with Feake, Rogers, Harrison and others refusing to support it. A further shared position among Fifth Monarchists was the illegality of the Protectorate, the target of their threats of violence, though the sort of government that they thought might replace it was a more open question, not least because of a degree of uncertainty among members as to whether Christ would himself return to reign in person, or entrust the rule of his kingdom to his saints.

What Fifth Monarchists did agree upon was that 'the elect' would have the upper hand in the new order, and use their authority to impose godliness on the masses. While in their ideal society there would be no state church, parochial system or tithes, morality would be upheld through a set of laws modelled largely on the Old Testament, complete (in the opinion of some) with the death penalty for adultery, blasphemy and Sabbath-breaking. In some respects, however, the law would be less severe than at present, with debtors no longer being imprisoned nor thieves hanged, and given their expectation of a 'mass conversion' when Christ set up his kingdom, Fifth Monarchists might not have anticipated much law-breaking in the new age. Their emphasis on 'the elect' involved a degree of 'turning the tables', since underpinning their sermons and tracts was a clear sense of the need for 'the oppressed' to be treated justly. In this they were at one with many of their contemporaries, and if Feake once declared that he wanted to see the aristocracy 'sit bare-breeched upon hawthorn-bushes' he might have sounded like a Ranter or Quaker. Like Quakers and Diggers, Fifth Monarchists often upset their superiors by refusing to do 'hat honour' and addressing them as 'thee' and 'thou'. The preacher at John Simpson's funeral in 1663 may have echoed the sentiments of many former Fifth Monarchists when he claimed that 'a nation is more beholding to the meanest kitchen maid in it that hath in her a spirit of prayer, than to a thousand of her profane swaggering gentry'.

Yet society under the Fifth Monarchists would not have been egalitarian. While they attacked social inequality and mocked the upper classes – 'corrupt naughty nobles' John Rogers called them, declaring nobility 'but a fancy for children and fools' – they appear to have envisaged, rather than a levelling out of status in the millennium, the elevation of themselves to form a new upper class: 'theirs was equality among believers only', as Christopher Hill puts it.[6] John Spittlehouse explicitly spoke of 'our new built aristocracy', John Simpson expected the saints to appear as kings, and Anna Trapnel prophesied that God would make them earls and potentates. Somewhat dangerously, Spittlehouse and others claimed to draw inspiration from the Anabaptists who took over the city of Münster in the 1530s and who were ruled over by the 'messianic' John of Leiden and his 12 'dukes'.

Despite the claims of their detractors, who saw their relentless attack on tithes as the thin end of an egalitarian wedge, Fifth Monarchists had no commitment to common ownership and publicly affirmed their support of the principle of private property. They did promote certain land reforms to ensure a fairer system for the poor, and took seriously Old Testament texts suggesting that a godly society was characterized by the absence of beggars; but if they wanted an end to poverty and begging they did not, unlike the Diggers, see 'owning all things in common' as the way to do it – though Venner's rebel group did speak of seizing and sharing out the possessions of all who opposed them. Cromwell once accused Fifth Monarchists of claiming 'that liberty and property are not the badges of the kingdom of Christ'.

As Capp has pointed out, many of the Fifth Monarchists' economic ideas and predictions reflected the interests and prejudices of the people they mainly represented, the artisans and small traders.[7] They attacked monopolies and merchants, and seem to have envisaged a world in which people could work unencumbered by the burdens they now endured in the form of taxes, tithes, rents, customs and excise, and unfair competition. Some of their ideas had an element of real-worldliness about them – increasing trade and production to generate more wealth, for example – but others were clearly rooted in a conviction that, once the millennium had come to pass, so the images depicted in Scripture of societies enjoying peace, harmony and prosperity would automatically come into being. Thus the anonymous writer of *The Banner of Truth* spoke of the saints enjoying immortality in the new age, Henry Danvers predicted that all would enjoy perfect health, and Mary Cary foresaw peace and prosperity being realized without hard work. Cary and others expected that Christ would 'chain up [the] devouring nature of the wolf and the leopard' and, as Isaiah envisioned, make the lion eat straw like the ox. But if some of these schemes were clearly fantastic, closely resembling the classical dreams of Arcadia and Cockaygne, Mary Cary does sound remarkably modern when she suggests – in words which not only echo Isaiah but anticipate Marx – that people would 'follow several employments as now they do', but 'not ... to maintain others that live viciously, in idleness, drunkenness, and other evil practices' but so that they might 'comfortably enjoy the work of their own hands'.

There was also a strong international dimension to the Fifth Monarchists' vision, a sense that what God was doing in England in bringing about the millennium would have implications for the rest of mankind. England was seen as the 'elect nation' which, as John Spittlehouse affirmed, God was using 'as a theatre to act as a precedent of what he intends to do in all the nations under the cope of heaven'. There was a certain logic to this, for if Antichrist, popery, was to be defeated, the battle had to extend across Europe.

'The blade of the sword (whose handle is held in England) will reach to the very gates of Rome ere long', claimed John Rogers, who, like many, saw the army having a duty to take up the cause and, in the process, liberate their fellow Protestants suffering oppression in Europe: 'To the other side of the water, away sirs!' he encouraged the troops, 'and help your brethren beyond the seas.'

Behind this concern was a belief that, in the last days, God would raise up a great emperor who would bring peace and unity to Europe and prepare the way for King Jesus – a role which many in the 1650s (including Andrew Marvell, who composed an ode to that effect) saw as falling upon Cromwell. Those who pictured Cromwell as the new Moses certainly envisaged his liberating work extending beyond England, and, in urging him to undertake a crusade across Europe, John Rogers reminded the Protector of an ancient prediction suggesting that his name would one day be heard 'within the walls of Rome'! Against this background, Cromwell's attempts to make peace with the Dutch might have been welcomed by Fifth Monarchists as drawing on side a Protestant ally in the crusade, yet in fact they keenly supported the war. The line that Feake, Rogers and others promoted was that the Dutch tolerated Arminianism and were a 'treacherous, self-seeking and ungrateful' people, yet Venner may not have been alone in recognizing that the Dutch cloth industry posed a serious threat to the interests of cloth-workers and weavers such as themselves, and the war as an opportunity to see off their rivals. 'The Dutch must be destroyed; and we shall have an heaven on earth' one Fifth Monarchist preacher is alleged to have said. In her trance in January 1653 Anna Trapnel was reported to have prayed against the outbreak of 'an ungodly and wicked peace with the Dutch, to the dishonour of God, and hindrance of the carrying on of God's work'.

What was the overall impact of the Fifth Monarchy movement? In terms of the support it attracted, the most reliable authority suggests that its numbers never rose above 10,000,[8] though since both its leaders and its detractors were prone to overestimate their size, the one to impress and the other to alarm, it is possible that this is wildly out. Feake went so far as to suggest, in 1655, that the movement numbered 40,000, and in 1659, between Cromwell's death and the Restoration, a report said they had 20–30,000 'armed men', with 5,000 assembled in the Sussex town of Horsham alone. Powell boasted in 1655 that he could produce 20,000 armed supporters in Wales, but the total number of signatures he secured for his petition *A Word for God* that year was just over 300. Fifth Monarchists were certainly much stronger in the south than the north, and in towns rather than the countryside (except in Wales), with London being by far the main centre of their activity.

Despite accusations from their opponents that they were 'the scum, and very froth of baseness', Capp's research has shown that among their leadership were several army officers and chaplains; a number of clergy; at least two navy commissioners; and even the clerk to the treasurer of the navy, the deputy treasurer to the fleet and secretary to the generals at sea, and the sometime chairman of the Admiralty Committee, Sir Henry Vane. Powell, Carew and Danvers were educated at Oxford and Feake and Rogers at Cambridge, and Carew (son of Sir Richard), Major John Bawden (who supported Anna Trapnel during her tour of Cornwall) and Danvers were officially 'gentlemen'. Among the Fifth Monarchist rank and file could be found a significant number of clothworkers and other craftspeople – around a third of their known membership were involved in the manufacture and distribution of cloth and leather – though they also attracted many from the bottom strata of society, including apprentices and journeymen. To judge from the membership lists that are extant, women easily outnumbered men, which makes the title by which they are usually known, 'Fifth Monarchy Men', somewhat unfortunate!

Despite the smallness of their numbers – even if Feake's figure of 40,000 members is accurate they represented less than 1 per cent of the population – they posed a considerable threat to Cromwell during the 1650s. They worked hard to sow discontent among the army – upon whose support the Protectorate depended for its survival – and carried on secret negotiations with other disaffected groups to create as broad an oppositional alliance as possible. That Cromwell had continually to resort to purging the army of those he considered unsafe is some measure of the effectiveness of their campaign, as is the fact that, as Protector, he had to live constantly under the threat of assassination. Several attempts were in fact made on his life, and he felt himself to be particularly vulnerable following the publication in 1657 of *Killing Noe Murder*, a tract which marshalled reasons from Scripture and Greek philosophy why tyrants needed to be killed in the interests of the people. Fifth Monarchists in fact denied responsibility for this tract (it was most likely written by Edward Sexby under his pseudonym William Allen), but some of their leaders did preach that taking the Protector's life would attract divine approbation, and the actions of Venner would not have allowed Cromwell to believe that they were 'all talk'. Cromwell's reaction to Anna Trapnel's 12 days of prophecy – moving to make it a treasonable offence to 'imagine the death of the Lord Protector' – suggests that he did not take lightly threats even from individuals with apparently no violent intent. Cromwell was particularly unsettled by the Fifth Monarchists' tactic of using biblical idioms to express their revolutionary intent, remarking on one occasion that 'they had tongues like Angels, but had cloven feet'.

What made Fifth Monarchists potentially more dangerous than their contemporaries who shared their millenarian outlook was the central place they gave to the doctrine and commitment to make it a reality at any cost, including, apparently, by force. The unrest that they were able to arouse was in part a consequence of the flow of events in the 1640s which kindled millenarian hopes across the board, but their leaders were skilled in being able to channel those hopes into a movement of protest and dissent by seeking to label Cromwell and Parliament as apostates and betrayers of the cause for which the saints had fought. As Capp quite reasonably concludes, the furore they produced was not a consequence of their millenarian ideas as such, but of their having 'developed a potent and dangerous synthesis in which these ideas became the justification for violent political action and sweeping social changes'.[9] This having been said, much of their talk of violence and the right to take up arms against Cromwell was just that, though they did harbour a minority which was prepared not just to sanction the death of the Protector, but, like Venner, literally to fight for the kingdom of Christ. Ironically the chief effect of their threats and warnings – when heightened by their opponents' claims that they were raising armies, planning massacres and plotting anarchy – was to contribute to the belief, increasingly widespread by the late 1650s, that there could be no peace and order in society until the king was restored.

Behind this lies the question of how much store they laid by 'human agency' in effecting the change they looked for, and how much they thought it would ultimately come about by divine intervention. The petition produced by Norfolk Fifth Monarchists in February 1649 – the first real statement of the movement's intent – asserts plainly that the 'kingdom and dominion' of Jesus Christ, which 'is to be expected about this time we live in ... shall not be erected by human power and authority, but Christ by his spirit shall call and gather a people [to] rule the world... till Christ come in person'. Linked to this, as Glenn Burgess points out, is the very limited significance Fifth Monarchists attached to 'politics', which is basically reduced, for them, to a 'holding pattern awaiting God's final intervention in human affairs'. Even when the Norfolk Fifth Monarchist John Tillinghast points out in 1655 that the saints are not to wait upon God 'as idlers do for help in a ditch, and cry God help us', in then affirming that 'we are to wait *as if* we would have it by our very striving and struggling' (italics added) he does not imply a profound faith in human action to achieve the desired result. For at least some Fifth Monarchists, as Burgess suggests, 'there was no sense ... that political activity was worthwhile in itself'.[10]

Despite flirting, in the mid-1650s, with the idea of supporting royalist conspirators to secure their aims, the Restoration was a huge disappointment for the Fifth Monarchists. Not only had their prophecies not materialized during the years of the republic, now they were to witness the disappearance of the few remaining benefits from the overthrow of Charles I. Of all the radical groups, they remained most consistently opposed to the Restoration in the

1660s, but they were to become increasingly a spent force – and, indeed, a *lone* force as Baptists and Quakers hastened to accentuate the clear blue water between themselves and Venner and the remaining Fifth Monarchists. Splits in 1657 had divided Feake and his more militant followers from Simpson and a more 'moderate' wing, and Venner's abortive uprising that year showed the movement's ability to cause alarm but not political change. Anna Trapnel continued denouncing Cromwell (and some of her Fifth Monarchist associates such as Venner and Simpson) through prophecy and preaching until the end of 1659, when, astonishingly, some 50 of her prophecies were published in two volumes totalling more than 1,000 pages; and the millenarian hopes of some were kept alive by suggestions that the esoteric numbering in Daniel and Revelation might point to the return of Christ in 1666 (a popular date given its close correspondence to the number of the Beast) or even 1701 (discerned by adding the year of the destruction of the Temple, 366, to the 1,335 'days' of Daniel 12.12). But the return of strict censorship with the Restoration, and a ban on religious meetings outside of the established church, sent the movement underground and silenced its presses. Venner produced a pamphlet in 1661 which had echoes of Sexby's earlier tract, and then led 50 followers on horseback in a second attempted rising in London; but the authorities' response – both he and his co-leader were hanged, drawn and quartered and then displayed in pieces on the city gates and London Bridge – indicated how future disturbances of this sort might be handled (Carew and Harrison had been tried and executed as regicides the previous October).

Their belief that ultimately it was God's prerogative to bring in the kingdom led many people after 1660 to see the Restoration as divine judgment on the country for 'backsliding': God had brought down king and bishops but had now allowed their return because leaders had used the opportunity to pursue their own private ends, a Fifth Monarchist said in October 1661. The plague of 1665 was also seen in this light. Danvers, Powell and others produced occasional tracts in the 1660s and 70s, but the expectation of any imminent change was lacking. Powell's *The Bird in the Cage*, published in 1661, suggested that the movement might adopt new 'survival' tactics under the new regime: the fifth monarchy had been 'unanswerably proved', Powell affirmed, but 'it is a great piece of prudence in an evil time to be silent'.

Fifth Monarchists continued to meet into the 1680s – we last hear of Feake preaching in 1682 in a cellar on London Bridge – and some might have pinned their final hopes on the Duke of Monmouth's rebellion in 1685. There is little evidence to show where the majority of surviving Fifth Monarchists went – few were prominent enough in society to have had their doings recorded – and the movement almost certainly did not survive into the 1700s. With a mixture of perhaps smugness and relief did the anonymous author of *Londons Glory, or, the Riot and Ruine of the Fifth Monarchy Men* ironically describe his subjects in 1661 as the 'never to be forgotten sect'.

CHAPTER SEVEN

Muggletonians

START TO READ a book or article on the Muggletonians, and the chances are that the author will begin by offering an explanation as to why he or she has expended time and effort considering such a seemingly obscure and inconsequential group, and why the reader might want to do the same. Treatises on, for example, the Diggers, are not thought to require such justification because it is assumed that they are better known, but it could well be argued, at least in terms of their size and longevity, that the Muggletonians should enjoy no lesser respect. After all, not only did they attract more popular support than did the Diggers, they outlasted them by more than 300 years! In fact the Muggletonians and Quakers were the only movements of those which originated in the mid-seventeenth century to survive into the twentieth; astonishingly, the person believed to be the last Muggletonian died only in 1979.

The name by which the movement is generally known is something of a misnomer in the sense that, although Lodowicke Muggleton led it single-handedly for almost 40 years, and undeniably played the major role in shaping the way it developed, the real genius behind it was his cousin John Reeve, also a tailor, who died within six years of its emergence. The origins of the movement certainly lie with Reeve who, in February 1652, received what he understood to be a special communication from God informing him that he and his cousin were the Two Last Witnesses referred to in the Book of Revelation. According to chapter 11 of that book, which records the dream of St John on the island of Patmos concerning the end of the age, one of the signs of the approach of the end will be the appearance of these witnesses. They are granted authority by God to prophesy for 1,260 days and their appearance will portend certain disasters leading up to the return of Christ and the end of the age. Reeve's 'commission', as he called it, was to be God's 'last messenger', with Muggleton as his mouthpiece – much as Aaron had been to Moses in the Old Testament account of Moses' encounter with God by the burning bush.

The relationship between Reeve and Muggleton has interested students of the movement, not least because there are signs that, while Reeve considered himself the more important of the two during his lifetime, his cousin sought to rewrite some of the movement's early history in later years to play up his own role and appropriate Reeve's legacy. Reeve records being prompted by the Holy Spirit, when being told that Muggleton was to be his 'mouth', to bring to mind the account of Moses' commissioning by God to represent his people before Pharaoh – and that narrative (in Exodus chapter 4) makes it very clear that Moses is superior to Aaron: 'he [Aaron] shall serve as a mouth for you', God tells Moses in verse 16, 'and you shall serve as God for him.' Was that how Reeve saw his relationship with Muggleton?

The evidence is far from clear. On the one hand, the cousins state in their apologia for their movement, *A Transcendent Spiritual Treatise*, that they are the Lord's 'two last witnesses and prophets', suggesting that the analogy with Moses and Aaron may not be worth taking too far. The *Treatise* also speaks of the Lord making Muggleton 'obedient with' Reeve 'in the message of the Lord' as Aaron was made 'obedient with Moses in the messages of the Lord at that time'. Yet Christopher Hill, noting that the *Treatise* is largely written in the first person as if by Reeve, and that his name appears in catalogues of the time as its sole author, has speculated that originally the wording had Aaron being obedient 'to' Moses, this being changed in subsequent editions after Reeve's death by Muggleton, who also appended his own name as the *Treatise*'s co-author.[1] Only two versions of the *Treatise* have survived, and although neither is dated, both do bear the names of both men, and in both the wording in the passage in question is 'obedient with'. Muggleton was certainly clear on the matter, and in his autobiography, *The Acts of the Witnesses*, published the year after his death, asserted that 'God did not choose *John Reeve* singular, but God chose us two jointly, so that there could be no separation but by death, and seeing God hath honoured me to be the longer liver, he hath given me a double power...'.

The purport of God's message to Reeve – which was spread over three mornings and spoken by 'the Lord Jesus, the only wise God' – was that he had been chosen to be God's 'last messenger for a great work unto this bloody unbelieving world': 'whoever I pronounce blessed, through thy mouth, is blessed to eternity', the Lord told Reeve, and 'whoever I pronounce cursed through they mouth, is cursed to eternity'. Specifically Reeve was told to denounce two of his contemporaries, Thomas Tany (also known as Theauraujohn, a name he adopted at divine command) and John Robins, sometimes described as a Ranter. Reeve had until recently been a disciple of Robins, a man apparently possessed of extraordinary charisma and magical powers and even greater pretensions to divinity – he was at the time imprisoned under the terms of the Blasphemy Act for claiming to be God the Father and that his wife was carrying the new Christ. Reeve was now to denounce Robins as 'the last great Antichrist or Man of Sin', along with his acquaintance Tany, who, according to Muggleton, had 'declared that he was to gather the Jews out of all nations and lead them to Mount Olives to Jerusalem'. In preparation for this task Tany had 'circumcised himself according to the law', and at the time of his cursing by Reeve he was making tents in readiness for an expedition to Palestine he was organizing.

The aspect of Reeve's calling that he believed set him apart from other prophets such as Tany and Robins – and, for that matter, more influential figures such as the Quaker leaders Fox and Nayler – was that it came from 'outside'. Whereas these others claimed that they received their insights from a revelation within themselves, Reeve's encounter with God was physical: he *heard* God speak to him audibly – as, of course, did Moses. In a comment on the eleventh chapter of Revelation, written in 1662, Muggleton makes a point of distinguishing between 'that which is by inspiration, revelation, vision or dream, and that which is given by voice of words to the hearing of the external ear'. The nature of God's disclosure to Reeve qualified him to be critical of, and even to 'correct' St John's revelation, since John, too, was merely another visionary, mystic and dreamer.

While there might seem little in Reeve's commission by way of a solid foundation upon which to build a movement, within a short while he and Muggleton had attracted a small following. They had also begun to receive mentions in periodicals and books, including the government newspaper *Mercurius Politicus* in 1653 when they were imprisoned under the Blasphemy Act, and the 1655 edition of Alexander Ross's *A View of all Religions in the World*. The end of the ages was still widely anticipated at that time, and the appearance of two people purporting to be the 'Two Witnesses' of Revelation would not have been an altogether surprising – or even unusual – occurrence. Two London men had aroused some interest in 1636 with their claims to be fulfilling that particular prophecy of Revelation, and numerous publications in the 1630s and 40s alluded to the witnesses, or, as in the case of Thomas Edwards' *Gangraena*, noted that their arrival was currently expected. Many who used their Bible to interpret the signs of times – and those who followed Reeve and Muggleton do seem to have been well-versed in biblical (and extra-biblical) teaching about the last things – would have been expecting them to materialize at any time, and, as Hill says, it would have 'seemed natural that they should appear in England and they should be Englishmen'.[2] The Antichrist or Man of Sin was also to be expected ere long, and for Reeve and Muggleton this clearly had to be Robins rather than, as many believed, the Pope, given his blasphemous claims and ability to show 'such signs as the Popes could never show, nor never shall show'.

While Reeve and Muggleton shared the widespread belief that they were living in the last days, they were not millenarians; for them the Second Coming would usher in the Last Judgment, the last stage before people went to heaven or hell, and they did not agree with those of their contemporaries who hoped that Christ would return to earth to set up and rule over – either in person or through his saints – a new kingdom of a thousand years. Initially it appears that Reeve thought that the end would come within his life-time – in 1656 he assured a follower that 'the Lord Jesus [will] make it evident that he hath sent us in a few months time' – but later he acknowledged that a much longer time span was required (though in 1674 a Muggletonian said that 'the time will not be long, for the lord's last prophets were two men who declared unto us that our Bridegroom is coming'). Whereas the millenarian Fifth Monarchists envisaged a special role for themselves in the reign of Christ on earth, the Muggletonians' conception of the new age envisaged no special function or position for the Two Witnesses: the saints would first participate in 'a spiritual reign or suffering with [Christ] for his truth's sake upon earth', and only 'when he appeareth in glory' reign with him to all eternity – and that not on the earth but 'in the third heavens'.

In common with a number of contemporary and earlier figures on the margins of the church, Muggletonians embraced the dispen-sationalist view of history known as 'the Everlasting Gospel'. This had been developed in the twelfth century by the abbot Joachim of Fiore, and was widely available in seventeenth-century England in the translated works of the mystic Jacob Boehme. Put crudely, Joachim advocated a 'trinitarian' understanding of history, dividing it into three main stages: first, the age of the Father, which was characterized by the giving of the law and spanned the period from the Creation until the end of Old Testament times; second, the age of the Son, the New Testament or gospel dispensation, the age of grace; and third, the final dispensation, which will come towards the end of the world and in which great emphasis will be placed upon the indwelling of the Spirit in humanity. For Muggletonians this third age, which they called 'the Third Commission', had been ushered in with God's message to Reeve and the appearance of the

Two Witnesses. Reeve described his treatise *A Divine Looking-Glass*, published in 1656, as 'the third and last Testament of our Lord Jesus Christ', and spoke of the prophets and apostles as 'my brethren'. For Reeve and Muggleton, as for a number of their contemporaries, from the time of the early church until their commissioning there had been no true prophet sent from God, and there would be no further commission until the end of the world when God will appear in judgment.

Muggletonians shared a number of core beliefs held by other movements: the right of the individual to discern the meaning of Scripture for him or herself without the 'aid' of a learned priest; the importance of the Spirit's teaching over the 'dead letter' of Scripture; and the 'sleep' of the soul between death and the Final Judgment (sometimes known as psychopannychism). Where they did stand much more on their own, however, was in a broadly predestinarian understanding of salvation, something they possibly shared only with Particular Baptists and most Fifth Monarchists. According to this doctrine, as articulated by St Paul and developed by St Augustine and, most famously, the Reformer, John Calvin, the eternal destiny of all humanity was settled before the worlds were made: God had 'pre-destined' some to salvation and (either by implication or design) the rest to damnation, and there was ultimately nothing an individual could do to change their eternal destiny.

In fact, Muggletonians (like Particular Baptists) may not have subscribed too rigidly to such a doctrine: as T. L. Underwood notes, there was a 'fluidity of definition' regarding Calvinism and Arminianism in the early Stuart period, and 'Muggletonianism, like other predestinarian creeds, allowed for both a voluntarist and a determinist vocabulary'.[3] Lawrence Clarkson, the sometime Ranter who became a Muggletonian and once challenged Muggleton for the leadership of the movement, was clear that God had 'prerogative power in matters of damnation and salvation' – but, crucially, what Muggletonianism did was take out the 'suspense' and apparently

'random' element in predestination by claiming that, as a consequence of the powers that God had given to Reeve and his cousin, it
was now possible for the individual to know whether or not he or
she was saved.

This was the significance of their appearance as the Two
Witnesses: hitherto people had not been able to know their eternal
destiny and hence had lived and died in despair; now, in this Third
Age or Commission, they could learn it from Reeve and
Muggleton. It was not the case that people who had no opportunity
to encounter the Two Witnesses were not saved, since salvation did
not require hearing their message; rather, such folk had missed out
on the opportunity to know *for certain* that they were saved, since,
with the coming of Reeve and Muggleton, it was possible both to
experience salvation and have assurance of it. Muggleton's belief
was that, in the final analysis, about half the world would be saved,
including all those dying in childhood.

The cousins' understanding of salvation was also behind their
reticence to evangelize: they spoke of their faith only when an
enquirer raised the topic, since while a person who had never met
or heard them might well be saved – though they were lacking in
assurance of it – a person hearing their message and then rejecting
it would inevitably be damned. Ignorance really was, more likely,
bliss. Thus a Muggletonian might discuss the faith with a complete
stranger who had made the first approach – a sign that perhaps the
truth might already be within them – but never with close family or
friends unless *they* happened to initiate the discussion.

As Reeve and Muggleton understood it, then, the human race
divided clearly into two: the elect, who were of the seed of Adam
via his son whom God favoured, Abel; and the reprobate, those of
the seed of Cain – who they held was descended not from Adam
but from a union between Eve and the devil. Both 'seeds' were at
work in each person, but the faithful were those who had more of
the good than the bad, more 'faith' than 'reason', and the damned
those in whom the proportions were reversed. The point was that,
by virtue of their being the Two Witnesses, Reeve and Muggleton
(and some of their followers) had the power and authority to recognize which was which, and to bless or curse accordingly. That

they may have held to a fairly flexible understanding of predestination could be argued from the fact that, in cases where the 'inner struggle' between the two seeds in a person might result in a significant change of behaviour, they were prepared to reverse an earlier curse or blessing (though as Thomas Tomkinson put it in his 'Epistle Dedicatory' to Muggleton's autobiography, this is not to say that God did not control the whole process).

For Reeve and Muggleton, the issue that determined whether a person was blessed or cursed was simply belief in themselves as the Two Witnesses. As John Gratton, who later converted to the Quakers, acknowledged, 'we had no more to do, but believe Muggleton, and be saved!' Neither Witness claimed the ability himself to *decide* a person's eternal state, only to demonstrate publicly what it was: their power was to recognize whether a person had a preponderance of the seed of Cain or Abel and pronounce upon them the blessing, or sentence of damnation, which already existed. But it was a power which both men exercised freely and with obvious satisfaction: Muggleton claimed that in his and Reeve's first ten years as Witnesses (Reeve, of course, only lived for six of these) they damned around a thousand souls. Blessing and cursing became for many observers a trademark of the movement.

While this practice of cursing and damning seems bizarre to the twenty-first-century mind, and indicative of what one might want to call extreme megalomania, it was not uncommon at the time. As Christopher Hill points out, some of Reeve and Muggleton's own opponents used it against them, including John Robins and the Quakers Josiah Cole and 'the saintly and cultivated' William Penn.[4] Penn's pronouncement against Muggleton was every bit as vicious as the man himself gave out: 'To the bottomless pit are you sentenced, from whence you came, and where the endless worm shall gnaw and torture your imaginary soul to eternity' – though Muggleton had the last word, allegedly retorting 'I care not a fart for him, nor his Friends!'

Cursing and damning also had certain social consequences in Reeve and Muggleton's milieu. Providing people with certainty about their salvation, an assurance that they were among the elect, was felt to have a considerable 'empowering' effect, and this could be enhanced when one knew that those who appeared to be the powerful in this world, who followed 'reason' rather than 'faith', would receive their just deserts in the next. Great solace was to be drawn from the knowledge that, however poor and insignificant one was made to feel in this life, those at the other end of the social and economic scale, the prosperous and proud, might ultimately be found wanting at the Last Judgment. And not only were things cashed out in the next world, for cursing the wealthy and powerful could have consequences in the here and now, including death and other misfortunes. One of the first people Muggleton cursed was a 'rich gentleman' who died within ten days, and, as he reflected later, this result 'was the more marvellous because it was never heard this many ages that a poor man should have that power, to bless and curse men and women to eternity'. There was something liberating, as a Muggletonian song put it, in seeing those that 'hath riches store ... crave for more' while 'I that am poorest of all, from worldly cares am free'.

In a hierarchical society like the one in which Reeve and Muggleton operated, cursing their opponents – those who offended against the Holy Spirit by refusing to recognize their commission as the Two Witnesses – was, as Hill has suggested, 'the supreme sanction for enforcing the prophets' authority, and their interpretation of the Bible'. It had a similar function to refusing to do 'hat honour' to one's 'superiors', though, as Muggleton delighted in pointing out to the Quakers he so despised, it was so much more effective![5] But it was also exercised against fellow 'radicals' whom the prophets did not like, including Quakers, Baptists and Ranters (some of whom might also attempt to get their own back). Thomas Tany, subject of the original curse from the Two Witnesses in 1652, drowned in a boating accident on the way to Jerusalem some years later, and Muggleton mentions two Quakers who died after being cursed by him, Thomas Loe and Josiah Cole, both of whom had also tried to curse him in language similar to Penn's. This was an age when people believed cursing had some effect: what is curious is that Muggletonians continued the practice until well into the nineteenth century.

Consistent with their 'predestinarian' understanding of salvation, Muggletonians held to a God who existed beyond them, a belief that set them apart from a number of their contemporaries. Ranters, Quakers and Diggers, for example, stressed God existing within the human heart, and laid emphasis on 'Reason' (Winstanley's preferred name for God) operating 'within', rather than faith in a God 'without'. Reeve explicitly rejected this, believing reason to be no more than 'desire' and the very antithesis of faith: it is 'reason' that prevents men and women comprehending God, that leads them to doubt that God could suffer and die and to underestimate God's power. Curiously, though, Reeve did understand the Devil in immanentist terms: 'there is no other Satan to tempt God or man but the motions and words that proceed from the seed or reason in man or woman'; the devil that tempts 'men and women to all unrighteousness, it is man's spirit of unclean reason, and cursed imagination, that unsatiably lusteth after things that perish'. Hell, similarly, 'is in a man, and not without a man', though earth might become hell after the Last Judgment. At the time of Reeve's commissioning God had told him that, if he failed to take it up, 'thy body shall be thy hell, and thy spirit shall be the devil that shall torment thee to eternity'.

If Muggletonians were not unusual in holding to a unitarian rather than Trinitarian understanding of God, in other respects their conception of the Creator was decidedly 'peculiar', in both senses of the term. The Muggletonians' deity was in some ways remarkably 'human', having been from eternity 'a spiritual body or person in the form of a man having all parts in immortality as man hath in mortality'. Perhaps not surprisingly this could admit of a rather literal understanding of anthropomorphic references to the divine in the Old Testament: 'If god had eyes, hands, head and back parts, must he not needs have a face?', asked Thomas Tomkinson in a debate with a Presbyterian sceptic. Some Muggletonians, including Muggleton himself though not Reeve, even wanted to give God measurements, suggesting that he was about the same height as the average human being. Muggletonians denied that they adopted such a concept of God because it might appeal more readily to ordinary folk, and it was certainly the case that the majority of their members were neither illiterate nor unlearned.

God the Creator was also, for Reeve, 'the man Jesus', who had a visible body. His (and Muggleton's) understanding of the Incarnation was that God, having entered into the womb of the Virgin and puri-fied her nature, exchanged his own immortality for 'pure mortality' and brought himself forth as, in a sense, his own first-born son. The Father, in other words, temporarily became a physical, mortal human, Jesus Christ, in order to identify with human beings, save them, and exalt them to his own nature. Following his physical and spiritual death on the cross, God then took on immortality again, and the Father and Son as one person ascended into heaven – which, unlike hell, was for Reeve an identifiable place above to which the elect will go after the resurrection.

This construct gave rise to complex, not to say abstruse, theo-logical questions such as who minded heaven during God's absence on earth, and to whom Christ prayed while suffering on the cross. Reeve's highly individual belief was that Moses and Elijah, who, according to Scripture had both been taken bodily up to heaven and later appeared to Christ during his Transfiguration, were made deputies for God while God lived among men. Reeve described Elijah as having been made 'the Protector of my God', an interest-ing use of a term with more immediate political connotations: indeed, on the title page of his 1656 treatise, *A Divine Looking Glass*, Reeve talks of Jesus Christ as 'Lord protector of Heavens' while also acknowledging that the dedicatee of that book, Cromwell, is 'styled Lord protector of England, Scotland and Ireland...'.

However Muggletonians pictured God, he was not one to take much interest in his followers on earth. 'God taketh no notice of his saints, nor doth not mind them at all', Muggleton once noted. Sceptics might seize on this, claiming that it ruled out any possibil-ity of gauging divine reaction to the Witnesses' words and deeds, and therefore of permitting any challenges to their 'authority'; but it did mean that faith would be kept pure, because one's motive for behaving morally was not hope of approbation from God, but belief that such behaviour was right in itself. If no God existed to reward the virtuous or punish the sinful 'yet could not I do any oth-erwise than I do', wrote Muggleton: the ultimate tribunal is 'that

149

law in my own conscience'. Those who do good simply because they feel 'God's eye' upon them only give 'eye service': this is discipleship based not on faith but on fear.

Yet Muggletonians agreed that there was one occasion when God did take notice of humanity – in 1652, when Reeve and Muggleton accepted their commission as the Two Witnesses. God's 'Infallible Spirit' clearly spoke to Reeve at that time, and God took 'immediate notice' of him and Muggleton when he gave them the power to bless and curse others. But this was highly exceptional, a rare example of people being subject to God's 'particular' providence, and when the cousins were not 'under the immediate testimony of the spirit' they were under God's 'general' providence, like everybody else. And in that state they had no special insights, which was why they could be some way out in their predictions regarding future events. An insight into God's 'particular' providence was not a possibility for humans, even by prayer: in fact God was not much interested in prayer at all and, as Muggleton once bluntly asserted, 'taketh no notice' of any offered by his saints.

৩৽৵৶

In the early days of the movement more than 40 per cent of Muggletonians were women, and the scope that the movement provided for women to participate, lead and write was doubtless a factor in its appeal. Ellen Sudbury and Ann Delamaine were regional leaders of the movement, as was Dorothy Carter of Chesterfield, who it can be inferred from Muggleton's writings was an active spokesperson for the movement. Indeed, it was largely due to the efforts of Sudbury, who was based in Nottingham, and Carter that the movement spread beyond London and established a base in the Midlands. Elizabeth Atkinson, a former Quaker, wrote two Muggletonian tracts in 1669.

Although Muggleton appears to have had good relations with women and, as is clear from his letters, empathized with their domestic concerns, it could not be said that he or Reeve went out of their way to make their teaching particularly attractive to women. Both believed that women had only been created to facilitate the generative process involving the two seeds, and Muggleton even mocked at women in movements such as the Quakers with their pretensions to preach (and was quite prepared to damn them if necessary). Even when writing to 'bless' a woman member, Muggleton could sound patronizing: 'John Reeve and myself, the chosen Witnesses of the Spirit, we having the commission and burden of the Lord upon us, We are made the object of your faith ... so that you shall be perfectly whole as to the relation to the fears of eternal death', he wrote to Elizabeth Dickinson in 1658; 'and your faith being in me, as the object in relation to the commission of the Spirit ... I do declare you one of the blessed of the Lord to all eternity.' And when it came to damning he seems to have reserved some of his worst invective for women – as Elizabeth Hooton, generally regarded as the first Quaker woman preacher, was to discover after clearly getting under the prophet's skin:

> *It is supposed that you are the mother ... to that Samuel Hooton of Nottingham, who was damned to eternity by me in the year 1662. It is no great marvel unto me that he proved such a desperate devil, seeing his mother was such an old she-serpent that brought him forth into this world ... She hath shot forth her poisonous arrows at me in blasphemy, curses, and words, thinking herself stronger than her brethren ... Therefore ... I do pronounce Elizabeth Hooton, Quaker ... cursed and damned, both in soul and body, from the presence of God, elect men and angels, to eternity.*

A Muggletonian hymn affirmed that in heaven we shall be 'all males, not made to generate, but live in divine happy state!'

That Muggleton liked to assume a 'father figure' role within the movement can be seen with respect to the close interest he took in how members conducted relationships with the opposite sex. Officially, marriage was an issue for members to decide upon for themselves, but Muggleton was not averse to offering advice on the topic, and thought that a marriage was most likely to last when the couple were matched in terms of age, status and religion. He was also known to match-make, and once wrote to a widow member of the movement 'introducing' her to a widower he knew, noting the latter's suitability in terms of age, his good nature and, particularly, his annual income, standing as a 'genteel trader' and possession of servants. If the lady were to take up his suggestion, Muggleton assured her, she 'may live in as much splendour and credit as any merchant's wife in London doth'.

༝ঞ

Muggletonians did not develop a coherent political philosophy, though they shared many of the concerns and aspirations on the 'radical agenda' of the 1650s. They were fiercely anti-clerical, seeing 'the fat-gutted priests' (as one of their hymns put it) as liars and hypocrites who treated the scriptures as 'merchandise' and sold heaven a bit at a time as people were able to pay them for it. The clergy were 'always teaching of God what he should do for his own glory, when indeed it is their own glory, in lusting after things that perish', Reeve and Muggleton affirmed. Priests were one of the 'unclean spirits' spoken of in Revelation 16.13 who live well by deceiving the people: they are 'ministers of the letter only, but call themselves ministers of the Spirit' and 'croaking frogs that keep the people in darkness, unto whom the people give their silver for nought'. The Witnesses' disdain for the clergy extended to other professionals, including lawyers, doctors and all who pursued academic learning. Since God preferred to speak directly to those 'of small account, and no reputation', scholarship was a futile pursuit, and Muggleton declared himself a graduate, not of Oxford or Cambridge, but the 'University of Heaven'. In one of his more outspoken moments he berated the legal system in England which denied the poor a fair hearing in the courts on account of their being unable to pay for it.

Muggletonians had little time for governments, viewing people who participated in them as of the seed of Cain and imbued with the Beast, 'the spirit or seed of reason' which 'hath the government of this world given into his hands' (Muggleton discerned the Lord Mayor of London to be one such!) Muggleton also had some sharp things to say about magistrates, yet neither he nor his followers were in any sense revolutionaries: from the start they were political quietists, constantly stressing their deference to rulers and willingness to obey the law (or suffer passively if they cannot obey), and rejecting the use of the sword on the grounds that it was wrong to slay those who were made in the image of God. Muggleton disliked Fifth Monarchists for their belief that the saints must bring about political change: it was the reprobate who would 'sack Rome' in these last days, he told them in 1665, and had not it been human reason, the Devil, which had showed Christ all the kingdoms of the world?

But if Muggletonians generally abstained from politics, there were some rulers that they clearly preferred to others – notably Cromwell, whom they saw as a 'faithful defender and deliverer of all suffering people' and an agent of God for the good of the country. In fact, Reeve regarded Cromwell as rather more than just another ruler, dedicating his book, *A Divine Looking-Glass*, in startlingly fulsome terms to 'most heroic Cromwell, who art exalted unto temporal dignity beyond the foreknowledge of men or angels'. Perhaps even more astonishingly, Reeve claimed to *know* that God has 'exalted' Cromwell 'into the throne of Charles Stuart' on the basis of his 'immediate commission from the Holy Spirit'. Clarkson, too, admired Oliver, writing the year after his death that, 'had it not been for the late Lord Protector, whose soul was merciful to tender consciences ... what a bloody persecuting day had been in England'.

Unlike Ranters and Quakers, Muggletonians experienced little hostility from the authorities, either before or after the Restoration. Occasionally they were brought to court for non-attendance at church or refusing to baptize their children, but such events were not common. Considering his notoriety, even Muggleton was not often in trouble, and although both he and Reeve were imprisoned for blasphemy for eight months in 1653–4, and Muggleton had scrapes with the law in 1663 and 1670, he was only punished once after he assumed the leadership of the movement on Reeve's death, for blasphemy and sedition, in 1677. Not that the authorities did not view him and his followers with suspicion: at his 1677 trial the judge recalled the zeal of those who had beheaded the king 30 years before and invited the jury to consider 'what design this villain had both in church and government'. (There is no evidence that either Reeve or Muggleton took up arms against the king, and Reeve disproved of Charles' execution on theological grounds.) Size may have been a factor here, as Muggletonians were a much smaller outfit than the Quakers, numbering never more than a few hundred compared to the Quakers' tens of thousands. They may therefore have appeared less threatening to the authorities, and the low esteem that they placed on regular meetings meant that they could generally avoid prosecution for holding irregular services.

They also managed to keep one step ahead of the law, Muggleton himself often avoiding trouble by moving from place to place and never staying anywhere long enough to draw attention to his presence. He was also adept at playing the system at its own game, and, when imprisoned in Newgate following his conviction in 1677, arranged for a follower to bring an action of debt against him so that he might be transferred to the slightly less uncomfortable Fleet prison! Muggletonians also survived by developing contacts with people and 'making unto themselves the friends of mammon', none more so than Thomas Tomkinson, who used the time-honoured method of buying drinks for the people that he thought he needed to keep sweet! 'A little money and friendship' was how he described his approach, noting how, on one occasion when a court appearance threatened, he met with the key officials 'and ended all for five shillings which was most of it drank'! Muggleton also differed from Quakers in eschewing suffering: rather than a state to be sought it was to be, at best, avoided or, at worst, endured. For just as God took no notice of prayers, so he was unmoved by suffering: nothing was to be gained by martyrdom.

The Muggletonians were never a large movement, they never proselytized, they hardly spread beyond their bases in London and the Midlands, and they damned as many as they blessed; how, then, did they survive until only a generation ago? Clearly one of the attractions of their teaching was the certainty and authority it gave to those who, for various reasons, lacked a degree of both: in highly uncertain and volatile times the truth could still be known because God had given it to his Witnesses, who demonstrated it by their ability to bless the elect and damn their opponents to destruction. At a time when it was widely held that God might speak to individuals, prophets who could prove that their message was authentically 'of God' by demonstration of God's power and 'signs following' were serious figures. Reeve and Muggleton claimed in their apologia *A Transcendent Spiritual Treatise* that God's first message to Reeve gave him an understanding of the Bible 'above all men in the world', and the authority that he and his cousin demonstrated in discerning the eternal state of their peers underlined their authority. Muggleton was under no illusion about his status: 'you all ought to be taught of me', he could claim, 'else you cannot be taught of God'.

The informality of the sect's structure may also have appealed to some, especially at a time when other movements were hardening into tightly organized denominations. Muggleton certainly thought that the movement's lack of 'bondages and entanglements which other sects do undergo' was one of its virtues. There is evidence that local Muggletonian branches, with recognized leaders accountable to Reeve and Muggleton, existed in a number of counties, and Muggleton allowed (and sometimes paid) a small coterie of second-tier leaders to write tracts for the movement. In a few areas there were arrangements for collecting a voluntary monthly contribution to the work. But, as Barry Reay notes, with their lack of ministers, relatively small numbers, and absence of concern about recruiting new members, 'the Muggletonians must surely have been the most informal of the sects in seventeenth-century England'.[6]

A further draw for some followers might have been the relaxed nature of the movement's meetings, which were more like gatherings for discussion in taverns and ale-houses than formal services. (The movement continued meeting in pubs and rented rooms until 1869, when they acquired a permanent reading room in the very part of London where Muggleton had lived.) Others, though, might have found the lack of action a turn-off – John Gratton, for example, after attending a Muggletonian meeting at Dorothy Carter's house, expressed his disgust that nothing happened apart from some meditation on the writings of the prophets – no 'preaching, praying or reading Holy Scriptures'. Observance of the Sabbath was not required, and since the only requirement for salvation was belief in the commission of Reeve and Muggleton, regular meetings for worship or teaching were considered unimportant. Muggleton in fact thought that, as long as members retained the movement's core article of faith, it would not matter if meetings were never held. As people living in 'the age of the spirit' Muggletonians held that all 'outward' or 'visible forms of worship' such as preaching, liturgy, prayer and even, apparently, Scripture reading were irrelevant, though they did sing their own hymns, many of which were paeans of praise to the Two Witnesses, to the tunes of popular songs. One report of their meetings simply states 'we spent some time in discourse, and then parted'. Muggleton recognized that individual members might find consolation in private prayer and so declined to forbid it, even though he knew God would ignore it.

The lack of emphasis within the movement on rules and discipline must have been a refreshing change for some, though Muggleton was not averse to the occasional excommunication – especially when members questioned his authority or, in the case of Lawrence Clarkson, attempted to undermine his position. Clarkson had the temerity to claim that he, rather than Muggleton, had been chosen by Reeve to be his 'fellow-labourer in the work of the Lord with him'; and although Muggleton did not damn him – he had not, after all, committed the unforgivable sin of denying God's commission to Reeve – he declared Clarkson 'excommunicated for ever' (and for good measure his wife, 'that venomous serpent ... cursed and damned to eternity').

Their belief in the futility of unnecessary suffering – which Christopher Hill argues reflects the Ranter origins of both Muggleton and Reeve[7] – was perhaps another reason for the movement's survival: while Quakers and Baptists might endure persecution for adhering to their principles, Muggleton allowed his members to pay their tithe if they wished and to conform to the church in other respects. 'Occasional conformity' was a not uncommon practice across society in the Restoration years, and Muggletonians appear to have been prepared to attend church just often enough to maintain their position in society and keep out of trouble.

Muggleton also toned down the cursing when it seemed politic to do so, and significantly did not curse the judge who fined him 500 pounds and had him pilloried in 1677. He was also shrewd enough to do a thorough editing job on Reeve's writings before they were republished after 1660, taking out, for example, references to 'heroic' Cromwell's role as God's agent in the downfall of the 'Jesuitical House of Stuart', and descriptions of supporters of Charles II as 'spiritual rebels against the everlasting God'! Whereas Reeve had suggested to Alice Webb in 1656 that God would visibly confirm his choice of the Two Witnesses within 'a few months', Muggleton removed any hint of a timeframe for the fulfilment of Revelation.

As a leader Muggleton was, as Hill delightfully puts it, 'magnificently uncensorious of peccadilloes among the faithful so long as they remained sound on the one all-important issue',[8] and clearly he must take most of the credit for the movement's survival to the end of the century. He may not have had the originality of thought of Reeve, or have been the intellectual equal of Clarkson, but he was possessed of practical commonsense and good organizational skills, and was evidently able to command respect. By the time of his death in 1698 – having almost reached the age of 90 – he was known as 'the prophet' and the undisputed head of a sect which had taken his name.

Along with Quakers, Muggletonians were the only movement of those which originated in the 1650s to survive into the twentieth century. Despite ever decreasing numbers and a persistent refusal to seek conversions, Muggletonians continued to meet, dine and debate right through the eighteenth and nineteenth centuries and even into the twentieth. Although the authoritative *Chambers Encyclopaedia* had written the movement off as 'extinct' in 1881, following the publication of articles in the *Times Literary Supplement* in 1974 by historians Christopher Hill and E. P. Thompson mentioning the movement, Thompson was put in touch with a Kent farmer, Philip Noakes, who proved to be not only a believing Muggletonian but possessor of the movement's entire archive, which he had rescued during the London Blitz and stored in a barn. The recovery of these papers, now housed in the British Library, has shed an extraordinary amount of unexpected light on this small sect, and made close study of its origins, beliefs and practices possible – the most comprehensive so far being that undertaken by Professor William Lamont and published under the title *The Last Witnesses: The Muggletonian History 1652–1979.*

Whether Mr Noakes, who died in 1979, will prove to have been the Last Muggletonian may never be known, but he demonstrated in his conduct his fidelity to the Witnesses' original teaching and the reason why observers might wonder how the movement survived as long as it did; since they never asked him about it, Noakes never discussed his faith even with his immediate family, yet when two Jehovah's Witnesses called on him explicitly to discuss religious matters, he gave them a lengthy discourse on the 'Third Commission'.

Conclusion

IN HIS SELF-SERVING but otherwise pointless book, *Historians I Have Known*, A. L. Rowse expresses surprise at how much of his long and distinguished career Christopher Hill devoted to studying the sort of people we are considering here. Why did he bother so much with these 'loonies', he wants to know. Rowse's unreconstructed language aside, it's a question I've also occasionally entertained while compiling this book, not least as I've mused upon some of the bizarre theological constructs of the Muggletonians, or tried to fathom why a handful of Fifth Monarchists thought they could bring London to a halt just months after the Restoration.

There are, of course, many positive answers to Rowse's somewhat haughty question. On one level these groups and individuals should be studied simply because they are interesting and entertaining. They all provide a good narrative – as evidenced by the fact that some of their stories *have* been recast as novels (*Comrade Jacob* by David Caute, based on the life of Gerrard Winstanley), as plays (Caryl Churchill's *Light Shining in Buckinghamshire*, the title of a Leveller tract) as songs ('The World Turned Upside Down', Leon Rosselson's tribute to the Diggers) and as TV dramas (Martine Brant and Peter Flannery's *The Devil's Whore*, in which Edward Sexby and John Lilburne feature much); and they are considerably more colourful than some of their much better-known contemporaries. But they also help us to understand what William Lamont, in his history of the Muggletonians, calls 'the seventeenth-century mind'.[1] Even the study of a group so peculiar and preposterous (to the modern intelligence) as this, built entirely upon the claim by two London tailors that they were key figures in the 'last days' as described in the Book of Revelation, broadens our understanding of the past, of the way people looked at the world at a given time and responded to its dramatic twists and turns.

Rowse's problem with Hill is that he cannot see the point of studying what 'people at large' thought ('as if thinking of people who don't know how to think has any value!'); only the opinions of those who actually govern and have to find solutions to the real issues of the day matter. Such a view hardly needs rebutting, except to say that even if the subjects of this book might be the 'losers' of history, as classically defined, their history is not one of insignificance. As David Horspool writes in his study of English rebels over a thousand-year span, why should we not want to know the 'alternative histories' that people *wanted* to write as much as the more solid ones?[2] And Billy Bragg (whose recording of Rosselson's 'The World Turned Upside Down' brought it to a mass audience in the 1980s) makes the important point that being truly 'patriotic' involves understanding, not just the role in our history played by monarchs and a supporting cast of 'aristocratic admirals and generals', but the long tradition of struggle for our rights and freedoms, of which the groups considered here were a vital part.[3]

Studying the written legacy of the civil war and interregnum groups is also of enormous value. Professor John Carey's comment about the Ranter Jacob Bauthumley's *The Light and Dark Sides of God*, that it is 'immediately recognisable as a neglected masterpiece of seventeenth-century devotional prose',[4] ought to enthuse us to study other writings of the period also overlooked by the canon. A good starting point would be the tracts of Bauthumley's fellow Ranter Abiezer Coppe, whose utterly unorthodox style alone makes him fascinating to read, even before engaging with his blazing, sardonic, yet also faintly comic, text. Gerrard Winstanley's oeuvre, recently made available for the first time in its entirety in a scholarly edition, can also stand alongside the better-known political texts of his day, and his editors rightly compare him to 'the finest writers of that glorious age of English non-fictional prose' that included Donne, Bacon, Milton, Marvell and Bunyan.[5] The record of Anna

Trapnel's vision, *The Cry of a Stone*, or of Sarah Wight's ecstatic proclamations, takes us into the extraordinarily powerful genre of women's prophetic writing in the seventeenth century. Surely many of these are also 'neglected masterpieces' which deserve inclusion in the literary canon.

But perhaps the main reason that we still read the Levellers, Winstanley and other of their contemporaries today is, as politicians and campaigners often point out, because they 'raised and fought over ... many of the basic issues which we still debate today'.[6] If the re-enactment of the Diggers' occupation of St George's Hill in 1999 was largely symbolic, then what it symbolized was the fact that questions as basic as whether it should be lawful for land to be retained undeveloped while homeless families walk the streets are still unresolved. Even leaving aside the wider question of whether 'the earth' should *in principle* be 'owned' and traded by individuals or corporations or nation states – which Winstanley, of course, was not afraid to ask – issues as diverse as the right to roam, the building of motorways, land tax, land-use planning, the selling-off of school playing-fields and squatting are all manifestations of the basic concerns that the Diggers sought to address, namely how can the earth once more give sustenance to all her children. Perhaps the renewed popularity of 'allotmenteering' – a response in part to concerns about food miles, food security and food price inflation – is a sign that we still see digging as critical for our survival.

The core concerns of the Levellers – democracy, liberty, equality before the law – also remain central in every age. If many of their demands, including universal franchise, salaries for members of Parliament, frequent parliaments and the elimination of pocket boroughs have now been met, the questions of freedom of speech, assembly and conscience continue to be hotly debated. The question whether religious groups should be exempt from legislation enshrining equality of opportunity for all, regardless of sexual orientation – which provoked some of the most heated debates and protests of the Blair administration of 1997–2007 – is but one modern manifestation of an issue which concerned the Levellers and their contemporaries like Baptists and Quakers in the seventeenth century, freedom of religion.

The question of protecting parliamentary privilege is still as critical in the twenty-first century as it was when Charles strode into the Commons in 1642 in search of the five members he considered traitorous, and so is the debate about whether Britain should have a written constitution. Providing the framework for England's first constitution was, of course, a task Lilburne and his collaborators aspired to undertake, and, as the historian Tristram Hunt points out, 'what the Levellers posited nearly 400 years ago was precisely the kind of secular constitution guaranteeing freedom of conscience and speech alongside a sovereign parliament which many regard today as much needed political safeguards'.[7]

The Levellers' concern that liberty should be understood in a deeper sense than simply 'protecting the rights of the individual', that it should also take into account the interests of the wider society, has relevance to contemporary debates. As Melissa Lane, Professor of Politics at Princeton University, has pointed out, the Levellers' 'pluralist defence of liberty – in defence of a broad and inclusive social good as they understood it – has been replaced in our day with a neutral defence of liberty, isolating it from any wider or deeper social values': so while we are tempted to see defending liberty in terms of compiling a bare, neutral list of rights, and draw no distinction between the values which those seeking those rights want to promote (which may even include support of terrorism), Levellers lived and suffered for the very values which they sought to promote, using their liberty to argue for what they understood as the common good. As Lane has argued, the Levellers can help us to reconnect liberty with values, to find the grounds to differentiate between *defending* the liberty of all and *valuing* that liberty which is used to help rather than harm others. 'One unsung lesson of reflecting on the Levellers is that, while liberty unused is at risk of being lost, liberty used ... only for values which people do not respect or share is at risk of being devalued.'[8]

৩৽ৎ

Some of the (to our mind) more obviously 'religious' ideas people held in the mid-seventeenth century also continue to manifest themselves in various forms. The sense of being in the 'last days', which concerned groups such as the Fifth Monarchists, Muggletonians, Ranters and Diggers, among others, is alive and well today, not only in the form of sects regularly predicting the end of the world, but in a genre of writing which explores the struggle of those who will supposedly be 'left behind' on a godless earth after the removal of Christians at 'the rapture'. The latest in a line of US books premised on an assumption that we are living in the 'end times' – the most famous of which would probably be Hal Lindsey's 1970 attempt to link biblical prophecies to past and future events of the Cold War period, *The Late Great Planet Earth* – these volumes have sold in astonishing numbers, particularly in their country of origin. As Bishop Tom Wright says, the popularity of such books suggests an 'American obsession' with the imminence of the Second Coming, one which can have profoundly serious consequences when it leads, as the evidence suggests it has, to a widespread assumption that there is no point being concerned about global warming or other environmental issues if God is about 'to bring the whole world to a shuddering halt'.[9]

Of far more value would be a recovery of the biblical portrayal of the millennium in terms of the future transformation of *this* world – which Diggers and Fifth Monarchists, among others, understood very well. According to its creeds, the church has always understood salvation, not in terms of an escape into worlds beyond, but, as the doctrine of the resurrection affirms, 'the transformation of that destined to death to share the life of a renewed world'.[10] Of value, too, would be a rediscovery of how books such as Daniel and Revelation can, as truly 'apocalyptic' or 'unveiling' writings, provide tools both for an understanding of the nature of power and government and for resistance and opposition to unjust manifestations of them.

In his concern to understand how, for example, 'the Serpent' in his day represented the powerful network of forces – monarchy, judiciary, clergy, landlords – which acted to prevent a restoration of true community, Winstanley can be an insightful guide. The Book of Revelation strikingly depicts that conflict between the forces of good and evil which is a feature of every age, and can thus inform contemporary political discourse as readily as it did that in the seventeenth century. In the way that its author, John of Patmos, employed the image of the Beast from Daniel to depict the Roman power of his own day, so that symbolism may be used to critique and challenge the 'gods' of this or any other age.

This may be of considerable importance given the tendency of some Western leaders, following 9/11, to read off their response to the threat and reality of terror in the light of apocalyptic texts of the Bible: the depiction by some US politicians of their nation as 'the greatest force for good in history' waging war on 'the axis of evil' would be one egregious example. The category mistake here, as Michael Northcott has pointed out in his study of 'apocalyptic religion and American empire', is that, rather than providing a rationale for all forms of imperialism, 'the coded and symbolic language' of Revelation actually unveils the true nature of empires and speaks of their ultimate downfall in the light of the coming reign of Christ.[11]

The readiness of Fifth Monarchists and, to some extent, Diggers to tie their expectation of Christ's return to a particular historical moment, and appear to lose their ground for hope once that moment had passed, might lead us to dismiss millenarianism as, in the pejorative meaning of the term, utopian. Yet millenarianism is less about providing the wherewithal for 'predicting the future' than a call to live in a tension between the present and the future, the 'already' and the 'not yet'. The mark of the true millenarian, as Karl Mannheim has written in his classic study, is the ability to discern the present 'propitious moment' – the *Kairos* – as an opportunity to transform the world which must be seized: 'promises of a better world removed in time and space are like uncashable cheques'.[12] The imaginative power of the Book of Revelation, writes Christopher Rowland, lies in 'its challenge to the *status quo* and its evocation of a better world, all linked to a passionate concern for present responsibility'.[13]

❧

Studying the groups in this volume reminds us of the power of religious ideas to inspire political action. At one time there was a tendency among leading seventeenth-century scholars to play down the significance of biblical imagery and language in the writings of movements such as the Levellers and Diggers, to want to see them as essentially 'secular' and 'modern' in their attitude and driven only to use biblical terminology and idioms by the conditions of the time. Had people such as Winstanley lived 50 years later than they did, the argument went, they would probably have expressed their ideas in the language of rational deism, saving us the trouble of having to penetrate through their religious verbiage in order to discover the 'real' ideas beneath.

Today scholars are less inclined to the view that political ideas can be separated from the language in which they are expressed, and might see the attempt by those earlier historians to do this as partly the product of an ideological assumption about the potential of religion to inspire realistic political programmes. Now the possibility that sincerely held Christian convictions underlie the religious language of leading Levellers and Diggers seems increasingly to be given weight, and the fusing of (as we define them) 'religious' and 'political' principles in their writings generally acknowledged without demur. Thus Winstanley's understanding of the alienation of the 'poor, oppressed people of England' as at the same time economic, political and spiritual, and the Levellers' employment of, for example, both natural law and the doctrine of creation to develop their ideas about liberty, are more easily accepted as *prima facie* representing a coherence of view, and adding to the richness and depth of their writers' thought.

The tradition of religiously inspired political and social action aimed at overcoming oppression and promoting social justice continues to thrive. In one of his later books Christopher Hill noted 'interesting analogies' between seventeenth-century 'radical religion' and liberation theology,[14] and the similarities between the latter's potential to inspire movements for change in Latin America, South Africa and elsewhere in the 1970s and 80s, and the reading of Scripture which informed the activities of the movements discussed in this book, are indeed striking. Just as in the seventeenth century non-ordained men and women asserted their right to interpret Scripture for themselves, and came to radically different conclusions regarding its message from university-educated divines, so lay-people inspired by liberation theology have 'rediscovered' the political dimension of biblical themes such as salvation and liberation, and Scripture's emphasis on the kingdom of God as the culmination of human history. Recent global movements aimed at making poverty history, promoting fair trade and cancelling 'third world' debt also owe much of their momentum to individuals and organizations inspired by religious faith – the latter campaign drawing its inspiration from the 'jubilee' principle described in biblical passages such as Leviticus chapter 25 and Deuteronomy chapter 15.

Given the relevance that the Levellers, Diggers and others who 'stood for freedom' in the mid-seventeenth century continue to have today, it is surprising that they are not better known. One reason, of course, is that their period is not a core component of schools' history curriculum, and in consequence, as Tristram Hunt strikingly points out, 'the one part of our history that teaches the fundamentals of modern citizenship – democracy, toleration, equality – is being quietly abandoned'. As he pertinently asks, can we imagine French or American schools ignoring the 1789 Revolution or the Wars of Independence?[15]

Part of the solution might be to seek new ways to present an account of the period, and building the story around the personalities and movements in this book would certainly be one way in which to bring it to life. Those responsible for curriculum development may hesitate to go as far as Martine Brant and Peter Flannery, co-creators of the television series *The Devil's Whore*, who candidly admit to weaving 'fiction' into 'fact' to make their drama about the civil war period 'work'; but, as Brant says, the past must be brought to life if it is not to be completely lost, and humanizing it by 'embracing character and narrative', by 'cover[ing] the pill of history with the sugar of drama', can aid learning by helping students begin 'living the story'. The effect of her four-part drama, screened on Channel 4 in the UK in November 2008, was, Brant claims, to enthuse school children about a historical period which they sensed was significant but about which they had been taught very little.[16]

Yet in different ways the subjects of this book *do* keep alive. One legacy of the anniversary events of 1999 is that a memorial to the Diggers now stands in the vicinity of St George's Hill and at other sites in Surrey with which they had connections (these all being linked to form a 'trail'), and more recently a plaque has been installed in Cobham parish church acknowledging its links with Gerrard Winstanley. Two streets are also named for the Digger leader in Cobham. The Levellers are recalled every year at Burford on the anniversary of the shooting of three of their number there in 1649, and St Mary's Church, Putney, has a fitting memorial to the debates on democracy held there in 1647. These debates received considerable publicity in 2007 when they were voted the event in Britain's radical past best deserving a proper monument in a poll in *The Guardian* newspaper. Baptists and Quakers continue to flourish in many parts of the world, maintaining the core principles and practices of their seventeenth-century forebears, and there is a view within Quakerism that, since it is the sole institutional survivor of the radical movements which originated in England in the civil war and interregnum years, Friends have a special responsibility in honouring their heritage.[17] Despite there (probably) being no more followers of the Two Last Prophets to keep their movement alive, a project to make publicly accessible the entire Muggletonian archive, in a freshly typeset and typographically modernised form, was well under way at the time of writing.

There is of course a danger that, in seeking to make the 'radicals' of the seventeenth century better known, enthusiasts go to the other extreme and over-state their significance. As Edward Vallance has pointed out, *a propos* the Levellers, the fact that the transcript of the Putney Debates did not see the light of day until nearly 250 years after it was compiled, and little was known about either Putney or the Levellers in those intervening years, must temper our passion to describe that movement as pivotal to the development of democratic thought in Britain. They may have been even more influential in their day than is often recognized, Vallance acknowledges, but, despite the reputation that they have acquired in recent decades, 'there is scant evidence that their works influenced any subsequent radicals, whether in Britain, America or France'.[18] Much the same could be said of Winstanley, who also largely disappeared from view in the seventeenth century only to 'resurface' at the end of the nineteenth.

Vallance is concerned that, in seeking to offer 'an antidote to a heritage industry fixated on the lives of our kings and queens', those responsible for institutionalizing the Levellers as history's first 'democrats' or 'liberals' might simply be providing its 'radical' equivalent.[19] The same argument could be made with respect to the popular description of the Diggers as 'England's first communists', and clearly it does as great a disservice, to the groups themselves and the wider public, to inflate their importance as it does to minimize it. Yet even if the writings of the Levellers or Winstanley were not widely read or known about in previous centuries, that does not diminish the influence they might have today, nor the need to honour their contribution to our history, and the world of political ideas, in appropriate ways. And that influence might be observed in some quite unexpected places: one striking feature of the 'G20' world leaders summit in London in March 2009 was the presence of quotations from Gerrard Winstanley both on placards held by protestors congregating outside the meeting, and in the text of a public speech delivered by British Prime Minister Gordon Brown as a precursor to that very event![20]

And surely that is the point, for while it is important that the people and movements described here are remembered and honoured, of greater importance is that their ideas continue to be debated and acted upon. History, of course, will never forget 'the great and the good', the Charles Stuarts and Oliver Cromwells, those who held the levers of power and believed that they were changing the actual course of events: our groups, by contrast, still mostly populate its footnotes and appendices. But it is nonetheless sobering to reflect, as Tony Benn pointed out in an address at one of the earliest 'Levellers Day' gatherings at Burford, that while Cromwell's place in history may be secure, the ideas of some of those he ignored, opposed and silenced while moving to establish his Commonwealth have, in the event, 'shown greater durability than the institutional changes that he carried through in his short reign as Lord Protector'![21]

Notes

Introduction

1. Morrill, John, *The Nature of the English Revolution* (Harlow, 1993), p. 68.
2. Hill, Christopher, *The English Bible and the Seventeenth-Century Revolution* (London, 1993), p. 68.
3. Coffey, John, 'England's Exodus: The Civil War as War of Liberation', paper given at conference 'The Last of the Wars of Religion: A Salute to John Morrill', University of Hull, 12 July 2008.
4. Scott, Jonathan, *England's Troubles: Seventeenth-Century English Political Instability in European Context* (Cambridge, 2000), p. 270.
5. I owe this to reference to Stephen Copson; Richard Greaves thinks Bunyan was taken with Fifth Monarchists: Greaves, Richard, *John Bunyan and English Nonconformity* (London, 1992), chapter 8 (pp. 141–53) passim.
6. Hill, Christopher, *The World Turned Upside Down: Radical Ideas During the English Revolution* (Harmondsworth, 1975), p. 395; idem, 'John Reeve and the Origins of Muggletonianism' in Hill, Christopher; Reay, Barry, and Lamont, William, *The World of the Muggletonians* (London, 1983), p. 64.
7. Hughes, Ann, 'Approaches to Presbyterian Print Culture: Thomas Edwards' *Gangraena* as Source and Text' in Anderson, Jennifer, and Sauer, Elizabeth (eds), *Books and Readers in Early Modern England*, (Philadelphia, 2002) p. 102.
8. McDowell, Nicholas, *The English Radical Imagination: Culture, Religion, and Revolution, 1630–1660* (Oxford, 2003), p. 7.

9. Condren, Conal, *The Language of Politics in Seventeenth-Century England* (Basingstoke, 1994), p. 158.
10. Cooper, Tim, 'Reassessing the Radicals', *The Historical Journal 50*, 2007, pp. 247–8.
11. Burgess, Glenn, 'Radicalism and the English Revolution' in Burgess, Glenn, and Festenstein, Matthew (eds), *English Radicalism 1550–1850* (Cambridge, 2007), pp. 79–80. I do not agree with Burgess that the Diggers had no serious political intent as he defines it.
12. Vallance, Edward, *A Radical History of Britain* (London, 2009), pp. 13–14.
13. Hill, *The English Bible and the Seventeenth-Century Revolution*, pp. 196–7.

1 Baptists

1. McGregor, J. F. 'The Baptists: Fount of All Heresy' in McGregor, J. F., and Reay, B. (eds), *Radical Religion in the English Revolution* (Oxford, 1984), p. 26.
2. White, B. R., *The English Baptists of the 17th Century* (Didcot, 1996), p. 17.
3. Himbury, D. Mervyn, *British Baptists: A Short History* (London, 1962) p. 18.
4. Wright, Stephen, *The Early English Baptists 1603–1649* (Woodbridge, 2006), pp. 8, 34, 40; cf. White, *The English Baptists of the 17th Century*, p. 19.
5. White, *The English Baptists of the 17th Century*, p. 25.
6. Acheson, R. J., *Radical Puritans in England 1550–1660* (Harlow, 1990) p. 56.
7. Wright, *The Early English Baptists 1603–1649*, pp. 224, 218.
8. Gibbons, B. J., 'Richard Overton and the Secularism of the Interregnum Radicals', *The Seventeenth Century*, 10, Spring 1995, p. 69.
9. White, *The English Baptists of the 17th Century*, p. 87.
10. White, *The English Baptists of the 17th Century*, p. 90.
11. Bell, Mark, 'Freedom to Form: The Development of the Baptist Movements during the English Revolution' in Durston, Christopher, and Maltby, Judith (eds), *Religion in Revolutionary England* (Manchester, 2006), p. 199.

Notes

2 Levellers

1. Hill, Christopher, *The World Turned Upside Down: Radical Ideas During the English Revolution* (Harmondsworth, 1975), p. 114.
2. Dow, F. D., *Radicalism in the English Revolution 1640–1660* (Oxford, 1985), p. 31.
3. Vallance, Edward, *A Radical History of Britain* (London, 2009), p. 164.
4. Manning, Brian, 'The Levellers and Religion' in McGregor, J. F., and Reay, B. (eds), *Radical Religion in the English Revolution* (Oxford, 1984), pp. 81–2.
5. Dow, *Radicalism in the English Revolution 1640–1660*, p. 38.
6. Loades, David, *The Levellers* (Burford, 1999), p. 3.
7. Wootton, David, 'Leveller Democracy and the Puritan Revolution' in Burns, J. H. (ed.), with the assistance of Goldie, Mark, *The Cambridge History of Political Thought* (Cambridge, 1991), p. 441.
8. Wootton, 'Leveller Democracy and the Puritan Revolution', pp. 412–13.

3 Diggers

1. Rowland, Christopher, and Roberts, Jonathan, *The Bible for Sinners: Interpretation in the Present Time* (London, 2008), pp. 69–70.
2. Holstun, James, *Ehud's Dagger: Class Struggle in the English Revolution* (London, 2000), p. 393.
3. Gurney, John, *Brave Community: The Digger Movement in the English Revolution* (Manchester, 2007), p. 212.

4 Ranters

1. Friedman, Jerome, *Blasphemy, Immorality and Anarchy: The Ranters and the English Revolution* (Athens, OH, 1987), p. 74; cited in Hill, Christopher, *A Nation of Change and Novelty: Radical Politics, Religion and Literature in Seventeenth-Century England* (London, 1990), p. 188.
2. Corns, Thomas N., *Uncloistered Virtue: English Political Literature 1640–1660* (Oxford, 1992), p. 177.
3. Carey, John, 'Foreword' in Smith, Nigel (ed.), *A Collection of Ranter Writings from the 17th Century* (London, 1983), p. 1.

4. Smith, *A Collection of Ranter Writings from the 17th Century*, p. 18; Hill, Christopher, *The World Turned Upside Down: Radical Ideas During the English Revolution* (Harmondsworth, 1975), p. 206.
5. Corns, *Uncloistered Virtue*, p. 179.
6. Hill, *A Nation of Change and Novelty*, p. 184.
7. Hill, *The World Turned Upside Down*, p. 186.
8. McGregor, J. F., 'Seekers and Ranters' in McGregor, J. F., and Reay, B. (eds), *Radical Religion in the English Revolution* (Oxford, 1984), p. 137.
9. Morton, A. L., *The World of the Ranters: Religious Radicalism in the English Revolution* (London, 1970), p. 110.
10. Smith, *A Collection of Ranter Writings from the 17th Century*, p. 8.
11. Smith, *A Collection of Ranter Writings from the 17th Century*, p. 32.
12. Hawes, Clement, *Mania and Literary Style: The Rhetoric of Enthusiasm from the Ranters to Christopher Smart* (Cambridge, 1996) p. 82.
13. Carey, 'Foreword', p. 3.
14. McDowell, Nicholas, *The English Radical Imagination: Culture, Religion, and Revolution, 1630–1660* (Oxford, 2003), p. 111.
15. Dow, F. D., *Radicalism in the English Revolution 1640–1660* (Oxford, 1985), p. 70.
16. Morton, *The World of the Ranters*, p. 111.

5 Quakers

1. Barbour, Hugh, *The Quakers in Puritan England* (New Haven, CT, 1964), pp. 181–2.
2. Damrosch, Leo, *The Sorrows of The Quaker Jesus: James Naylor and the Puritan Crackdown on the Free Spirit* (Cambridge, 1996), p. 27.
3. Gill, Catie, *Women in the Seventeenth-Century Quaker Community* (Aldershot, 2005), p. 18.
4. Reay, B., 'Quakerism and Society' in McGregor, J. F., and Reay, B. (eds), *Radical Religion in the English Revolution* (Oxford, 1984), p. 145.
5. Nevitt, Marcus, *Women and the Pamphlet Culture of Revolutionary England, 1640–1660* (Aldershot, 2006), pp. 136–7.
6. Reay, B., 'Quakerism and Society', p. 151.
7. Barbour, *The Quakers in Puritan England*, p. 198.
8. Hill, *The World Turned Upside Down*, pp. 241–2.
9. Reay, Barry, 'The Quakers, 1659, and the Restoration of the Monarchy', *History* 63, 1978, p. 213.

10. Underdown, David, *Revel, Riot and Rebellion: Popular Politics and Culture in England 1603–1660* (Oxford, 1985), p. 252.
11. Smith, Nigel, *Perfection Proclaimed: Language and Literature in English Radical Religion 1640–1660* (Oxford, 1989), p. 9.
12. Reay, 'The Quakers, 1659, and the Restoration of the Monarchy', p. 213.
13. Reay, 'The Quakers, 1659, and the Restoration of the Monarchy', p. 212.
14. Hill, *The World Turned Upside Down*, p. 256.
15. Ingle, H. Larry, *First Among Friends: George Fox and the Creation of Quakerism* (New York, 1994), pp. 150–2, cited in Underwood, T. L. (ed.), *The Acts of the Witnesses: The Autobiography of Lodowick Muggleton and Other Early Muggletonian Writings* (New York, 1999), p. 6.

6 Fifth Monarchists

1. Cohn, Norman, *The Pursuit of the Millennium* (London, 1970), p. 13.
2. Capp, Bernard, 'The Fifth Monarchists and Popular Millenarianism' in McGregor, J. F., and Reay, B. (eds), *Radical Religion in the English Revolution* (Oxford, 1984), p. 171.
3. Morrill, John, *Oliver Cromwell* (Oxford, 2007), p. 80.
4. Capp, B. S., *The Fifth Monarchy Men: A Study in Seventeenth-century English Millenarianism* (London, 1972), p. 113.
5. Capp, 'The Fifth Monarchists and Popular Millenarianism', p. 170.
6. Hill, Christopher, *The Experience of Defeat: Milton and Some Contemporaries* (New York, 1984), p. 60.
7. Capp, *The Fifth Monarchy Men*, p. 148.
8. Capp, *The Fifth Monarchy Men*, p. 82.
9. Capp, *The Fifth Monarchy Men*, p. 20.
10. Burgess, Glenn, 'Radicalism and the English Revolution' in Burgess, Glenn, and Festenstein, Matthew (eds), *English Radicalism 1550–1850* (Cambridge, 2007), p. 77.

7 Muggletonians

1. Hill, Christopher, 'Debate: the Muggletonians', *Past and Present* 104, 1984, p. 154.

2. Hill, Christopher 'Why Bother About the Muggletonians?' in Hill, Christopher, Reay, Barry, and Lamont, William, *The World of the Muggletonians* (London, 1983), p. 17.
3. Underwood, T. L. (ed.), *The Acts of the Witnesses: The Autobiography of Lodowick Muggleton and Other Early Muggletonian Writings* (New York, 1999), p. 17.
4. Hill, Christopher, 'John Reeve and the Origins of Muggletonianism' in Hill, Reay and Lamont, *The World of the Muggletonians*, p. 74.
5. Hill, 'John Reeve and the Origins of Muggletonianism', p. 75.
6. Reay, Barry, 'The Muggletonians: An Introductory Survey' in Hill, *Muggletonians*, p. 35.
7. Hill, Christopher, 'Debate: the Muggletonians', pp. 158–9.
8. Hill, 'John Reeve and the Origins of Muggletonianism', p. 101.

Conclusion

1. Lamont, William, *Last Witnesses: The Muggletonian History, 1652–1979* (Aldershot, 2006), p. 248.
2. Horspool, David, *The English Rebel: One Thousand Years of Troublemaking, from the Normans to the Nineties* (London, 2009), p. xix.
3. Bragg, Billy, *The Progressive Patriot: A Search for Belonging* (London, 2006), p. 14.
4. Carey, John, 'Foreword' in Smith, Nigel (ed.), *A Collection of Ranter Writings from the 17th Century* (London, 1983), p. 2.
5. Corns, Thomas N, Hughes, Ann, and Loewenstein, David (eds), *The Complete Works of Gerrard Winstanley* (Oxford, 2009), pp. 65–6.
6. Benn, Tony, 'Foreword' in Brockway, Fenner, *Britain's First Socialists* (London, 1980), p. x, cited in Reay, B., 'Introduction' in McGregor, J. F., and Reay, B. (eds), *Radical Religion in the English Revolution* (Oxford, 1984), p. 20.
7. Hunt, Tristram, 'A Jewel of Democracy', *Guardian (g2)*, 26 October 2007, p. 7.
8. Lane, Melissa, 'Liberty as a Social Value: Lessons from the Levellers', talk given at the Convention on Modern Liberty, 28 February 2009, downloaded from: *www.opendemocracy.net/blog/ourkingdom-theme/melissa-lane/2009/03/11/liberty-as-a-social-value-lessons-from-the-levellers* (accessed 27 February 2010).

9. Wright, Tom, *Surprised by Hope* (London, 2007), pp. 130–1.
10. Rowland, Christopher, *Revelation* (London: 1993), p. 148.
11. Northcott, Michael, *An Angel Directs the Storm* (London, 2004), p. 75.
12. Mannheim, Karl, *Ideology and Utopia: An Introduction to the Sociology of Knowledge* (London, 1946), pp. 193, 196.
13. Rowland, *Revelation*, pp. 2–3.
14. Hill, *The English Bible and the Seventeenth-Century Revolution*, Appendix B, pp. 447–51.
15. Hunt, 'A Jewel of Democracy', p. 7.
16. Brant, Martine, 'I took liberties with *The Devil's Whore*', *The Observer*, 30 November 2008 (accessed 27 February 2010).
17. See, for example, McIntosh, Alistair, 'God, Creation and YM 2000', *The Friends Quarterly*, April 2000, p. 53.
18. Vallance, Edward, *A Radical History of Britain* (London, 2009), p. 201.
19. Vallance, Edward, 'The Levellers' Legacy', *BBC History Magazine*, October 2007, p. 38.
20. Text of speech at *www.number10.gov.uk/Page18858* (accessed 9 April 2009).
21. Benn, Tony, 'Leveller Spirit', *Guardian Weekly*, 23 May 1976.

Further Reading

General

Acheson, R. J., *Radical Puritans in England 1550–1660* (Harlow, 1990).

Bradstock, Andrew, and Rowland, Christopher (eds), *Radical Christian Writings: A Reader* (Oxford, 2002).

Dow, F. D., *Radicalism in the English Revolution 1640–1660* (Oxford, 1985).

Durston, Christopher, and Maltby, Judith, *Religion in Revolutionary England* (Manchester, 2006).

Hill, Christopher, *The World Turned Upside Down: Radical Ideas During the English Revolution* (Harmondsworth, 1975).

Hinds, Hilary, *God's Englishwomen: Seventeenth-century Radical Sectarian Writing and Feminist Criticism* (Manchester, 1996).

Hobby, Elaine, *Virtue of Necessity: English Women's Writing 1649–88* (London, 1988).

Holstun, James, *Ehud's Dagger: Class Struggle in the English Revolution* (London, 2000).

McGregor, J. F., and Reay, B. (eds), *Radical Religion in the English Revolution* (Oxford, 1984).

Smith, Nigel, *Perfection Proclaimed: Language and Literature in English Radical Religion 1640–1660* (Oxford, 1989).

Individual movements

Baptists

Haykin, Michael A. G., *Kiffin, Knollys and Keach: Rediscovering our English Baptist Heritage* (Leeds, 1996).

White, B. R., *The English Baptists of the 17th Century* (Didcot, 1996).
Wright, Stephen, *The Early English Baptists 1603–1649* (Woodbridge, 2006).
www.baptisthistory.org.uk
www.strictbaptisthistory.org.uk

Levellers

Aylmer, G. E., *The Levellers in the English Revolution* (London, 1975).
Brailsford, H. N., *The Levellers and the English Revolution* (Nottingham, 1976).
Morton, A. L. (ed.), *Freedom in Arms: A Selection of Leveller Writings* (London, 1975).
Sharp, Andrew, (ed.), *The English Levellers* (Cambridge, 1998).
www.levellers.org.uk

Diggers

Bradstock, Andrew, *Faith in the Revolution: The Political Theologies of Müntzer and Winstanley* (London, 1997).
Bradstock, Andrew (ed.), *Winstanley and the Diggers 1649–1999* (London, 2000).
Corns, Thomas N; Hughes, Ann; and Loewenstein, David (eds), *The Complete Works of Gerrard Winstanley* (Oxford, 2009).
Gurney, John, *Brave Community: The Digger Movement in the English Revolution* (Manchester, 2007).
www.elmbridgemuseum.org.uk/diggers/links.asp
www.tlio.org.uk

Ranters

Friedman, Jerome, *Blasphemy, Immorality and Anarchy: The Ranters and the English Revolution* (Athens, OH, 1987).
Hopton, Andrew (ed.), *Abiezer Coppe: Selected Writings* (London, 1987).
Morton, A. L., *The World of the Ranters: Religious Radicalism in the English Revolution* (London, 1970).
Smith, Nigel (ed.), *A Collection of Ranter Writings from the 17th Century* (London, 1983).

Quakers

Barbour, Hugh, *The Quakers in Puritan England* (New Haven, CT, 1964).
Davies, Adrian, *The Quakers in English Society 1655–1725* (Oxford, 2000).

Further Reading

Gill, Catie, *Women in the Seventeenth-Century Quaker Community* (Aldershot, 2005).

Mack, Phyllis, *Visionary Women: Ecstatic Prophecy in Seventeenth-Century England* (Berkeley, CA, 1992).

Reay, Barry, *The Quakers and the English Revolution* (London, 1985).

www.quaker.org

Fifth Monarchists

Capp, B. S., *The Fifth Monarchy Men: A Study in Seventeenth-century English Millenarianism* (London, 1972).

Muggletonians

Hill, Christopher; Reay, Barry; and Lamont, William, *The World of the Muggletonians* (London, 1983).

Lamont, William, *Last Witnesses: The Muggletonian History, 1652–1979* (Aldershot, 2006).

Underwood, T. L. (ed.), *The Acts of the Witnesses: The Autobiography of Lodowick Muggleton and Other Early Muggletonian Writings* (New York, 1999).

Conclusion

www.muggletonianpress.com

Index

Index